W9-BFP-777

Savannah à la Carte

A
Savannah Symphony
Women's Guild
Cookbook

Copyright © 1999
Savannah Symphony Women's Guild
225 Abercorn Street
Savannah, Georgia 31401

Paintings Copyright © 1998
Lawrence Levow
114 West Jones
Savannah, Georgia 31401

Library of Congress Number: 98-061164
ISBN: 0-9665025-0-7

Designed, Edited, and Manufactured by
Favorite Recipes® Press
an imprint of

FRP

P.O. Box 305142
Nashville, Tennessee 37230
1-800-358-0560

Cover Design: Steve Newman
Book Design: Bill Kersey
Project Manager: Judy Jackson

Manufactured in the United States of America
First Printing: 1999   7,500 copies

All rights reserved. No part of this book may be reproduced or transmitted
in any form, or by any means, electronic or mechanical, including photocopying,
recording, or by any information storage and retrieval system, without prior
written permission from the Savannah Symphony Women's Guild.

Contents

Introduction

Beautiful Savannah, settled in 1733 under the leadership of James Oglethorpe, is a city with a rich cultural tradition. To drive, or even better to walk, through the squares of the Historic District, with their moss-decked oaks and blazing azaleas, is to return to a past when cotton was king and square-riggers lined the wharves on the river. Savannah is a living museum of eighteenth- and nineteenth-century architecture—the Owens-Thomas House and the Scarbrough House, both designed by English architect William Jay; the Andrew Low House and the Juliet Gordon Low House, originally the home of Supreme Court Justice James Moore Wayne and later the birthplace of the founder of the Girl Scouts; and the Isaiah Davenport House, a Federal-style mansion saved from the wrecker's ball by the seven women who founded the Historic Savannah Foundation. All these museum houses and many of the city's restored private residences boast rare collections of antique furniture and artifacts. Many have hidden gardens of floral charm, some visible through wrought-iron gates.

Savannah is a city devoted to the visual and performing arts. The Telfair Academy of Arts and Sciences, the oldest art museum in the Southeast, has a rich collection of American Impressionist paintings. The Savannah College of Art and Design has trained thousands of talented young people in painting, sculpture, architecture, and historic preservation. Contemporary artists are represented in the numerous galleries scattered throughout the Historic District. The people of Savannah love their theatre. City Lights features a series of comedies and thought-provoking dramatic productions as well as an annual outdoor Shakespeare performance. The Savannah Theatre has a history dating back to the early nineteenth century. The Asbury Memorial Theatre offers fine presentations of popular musicals. The Lucas Theatre, when renovated, will enhance the cultural life of the city.

Savannah has a strong musical tradition. It is the city of Johnny Mercer, of Emma Kelly, the lady of 6,000 songs, and of Ben Tucker, who joyfully accompanies her on the bass when he is not performing with his own ensemble. Each spring some of the country's finest young vocalists enter the American Traditions Competition, a highlight of the Savannah Onstage International Arts Festival, which also includes chamber music concerts, solo instrumental performances, and jazz. National touring companies, including the New York City Opera, bring the arias of Bizet, Puccini, and Verdi to the Savannah Civic Center. From time to time, a ballet company will come to town, even the world-renowned Bolshoi Ballet. Savannahians love to sing, as evidenced by the number of men and women participating in church choirs, barbershop groups, the Savannah Symphony Chorus, and I Cantori, Savannah's professional choral ensemble.

The core of Savannah's musical life is the Savannah Symphony Orchestra. Founded in 1953 as a community orchestra, it has achieved a national reputation and has been named the number one music organization in the state by the Georgia Council for the Arts. Its world-class musicians are led by Maestro Philip Greenberg, who has served as Music Director and Conductor since 1985. Each season the orchestra presents nine Masterworks

Concerts, featuring music by the great classical composers. Some of the world's greatest virtuosos have performed with the orchestra—Yo Yo Ma, Itzhak Perlman, Isaac Stern, Andre Watts, and Pinchus Zuckerman to name but a few. The Savannah Pops, with Skitch Henderson as its principal conductor, offers lighter musical fare and has featured such renowned performers as Victor Borge and Doc Severinson. Chamber orchestra concerts are presented at the Telfair Academy, at The Landings, and on Hilton Head Island. The Black Heritage Concert has become a Savannah tradition. Free concerts are offered to the community in Forsyth Park and as part of the Arts on the River Festival. String, wind, and brass ensemble demonstrations and concerts for young people provide encouragement in music appreciation to more than 10,000 children in the Chatham County public schools. All told, the symphony offers more than 300 performances each year.

The Savannah Symphony Women's Guild is devoted to providing financial support for the symphony. The dedicated women who participate in Guild activities organize fund-raising events in furtherance of the symphony's programs. Each September the Guild produces a two-day televised auction at the WJCL-TV studios. It presents the popular Champagne Events, a luncheon and a gala black-tie dinner, both featuring a spectacular fashion show with members of the Guild as models. A spring fashion show is held each year as a tribute to "Women on the Go." The Guild organizes the Savannah Duck Race, a fun-filled event held each May in which numbered rubber ducks float down the Savannah River at the turn of the tide, with prizes awarded to the holders of tickets corresponding to the winning ducks.

Savannah is a city of mouth-watering food as well as melodious music. PARTIES A LA CARTE, a series of elegant parties at private homes and other selected venues, is an important fund-raising event for the Guild and the inspiration for the serenade of menus and recipes presented here. Conceived in 1986, PARTIES A LA CARTE offers the best of southern hospitality in the form of black-tie dinners, jazz brunches, oyster roasts, low-country boils, teas, and fashion shows. The brochure of events is eagerly awaited each year by those friends of the symphony who appreciate the flavors of France, Italy, and the lands South of the Border as much as they appreciate a Mozart concerto or a Gershwin melody. A group of hosts and hostesses sponsors each event, and the guests pay a set charge that flows directly to the symphony. Good conversation and laughter accompany the exquisite fare provided by chefs from Savannah's finest restaurants or by amateur cooks eager to display their culinary skills.

In the belief that a fine meal, beautifully presented, can provide a symphony of taste and aesthetic pleasure almost as sublime as a symphony by Beethoven or Brahms, the Savannah Symphony Women's Guild is presenting this medley of taste treats from the recipe files of Guild members and other music lovers who believe that good food can be music for the soul. "If music be the food of love, play on," said Orsinio, Duke of Illyria, in the opening act of *Twelfth Night*. "If food be the music of life, read on," say we.

Acknowledgments

Enablers

Antiques courtesy of:
Carson Davis, Ltd., Savannah, Georgia
Pierce Antiques, Savannah, Georgia

Musical instruments courtesy of:
Portman's Music, Savannah, Georgia
Special thanks to Vernon Ricord

Photographs of original artwork:
Erwin Gaspin
Lorraine Jones

The Cookbook Committee

Dian Brownfield	Jane Kahn
Penny Dulaney	Fran Levow
Camille O'Neill Farrow	Larry Levow
Kathleen Henry	Joan Levy
Gloria Horstman	Margie Levy
Charles Johnson	Anna Nichols
Chris Johnson	Rose Williams

About the Artist

Lawrence Levow is primarily a self-taught artist, although his education and career have both been in the design field. As an industrial designer for over thirty years, he has designed literally hundreds of products, packages, exhibits, and corporate logotypes for major American and foreign companies. His designs have won national awards; he is the recipient of several patents and has been listed in *Who's Who In Corporate Identity*.

In 1994 he decided to concentrate on his first love—painting in pastels and oils. Since that time his work has been in a number of group and solo exhibitions and has been acquired for both corporate and private collections.

Mr. Levow is a faculty advisor at The Savannah College of Art and Design, where he teaches part-time. He exhibits at both Signature Gallery and Gallery 209 in Savannah, Georgia, and at the Caribbean Gallery in Key West, Florida.

Mr. Levow resides and paints in the Historic District of Savannah.

Picnics in the Park
...and on the River

Music lovers look forward each year to the Picnic in the Park, the occasion for a supper under the stars in Forsyth Park accompanied by the strains of the Savannah Symphony Pops Orchestra. Out come the fine linen tablecloths and silver candelabra to vie for the most beautiful table setting award. The melodies of Bernstein and Gershwin fill the fall air to accompany plates of fried chicken, pasta salad, and ratatouille, washed down by a simple beaujolais.

Another occasion for alfresco dining is the Arts on the River Concert, performed each spring on the Savannah River. Friends gather as the sun sets to sip a glass of sangria and munch on nachos before attacking the potato salad and peel-'em-yourself shrimp. Bats fly overhead as darkness falls, and a container ship from far-off Greece may slip upriver to Port Wentworth. It is a tradition on these occasions for the orchestra to play the *1812 Overture*, accompanied by the guns of Fort Stewart. Fireworks follow, and the evening ends with a stirring rendition of "Stars and Stripes Forever." When thoughts turn to the outdoors, remember, too, the traditional oyster roast and low-country boil, featuring the succulent seafood that abounds on the Georgia coast.

Levon '98

Contents

Menu

Rhapsody on the River

Roasted oysters

Overnight Barbecued Chicken
(page 12)

Barbecued pork

Brunswick Stew
(page 13)

Wild Rice Imperiale
(page 76)

Coleslaw

Johnny Harris' Mud Pie
(page 12)

Johnny Harris' Mud Pie

1 graham cracker pie shell
1/2 gallon coffee ice cream, softened
1 (8-ounce) jar fudge topping
1 cup chopped pecans
1 can whipped cream
1 squeezeable bottle chocolate syrup

Fill the pie shell with the ice cream. Freeze for 1 hour or until firm. Spread the fudge topping over the ice cream. Freeze until firm. Top each serving with pecans, whipped cream and chocolate syrup.

Yield: 6 to 8 servings

Overnight Barbecued Chicken

2 chickens, cut up
1/2 cup wine vinegar
1/4 cup Worcestershire sauce
1/2 cup water
1 1/2 cups packed brown sugar
1 1/2 cups catsup

2 teaspoons salt
1 1/2 teaspoons pepper
2 1/2 tablespoons dry mustard
2 teaspoons paprika
2 dashes of hot pepper sauce

Combine the chicken with 2 inches of water in a large saucepan. Cook, covered, for 30 minutes; drain well.

For the marinade, combine the vinegar, Worcestershire sauce, 1/2 cup water, brown sugar, catsup, salt, pepper, dry mustard, paprika and hot pepper sauce in a blender container. Process until mixed. Remove and reserve 1 cup of the marinade; store in the refrigerator until grilling time.

Place the chicken in a deep pan or dish. Pour the remaining marinade over the chicken. Marinate, covered, in the refrigerator overnight.

Remove the chicken from the marinade, discarding the remaining marinade. Grill the chicken until the skin is browned and crisp and the chicken is cooked through.

Simmer the reserved marinade in a saucepan for 5 minutes or until heated through. Serve with the chicken.

Yield: 8 servings

Brunswick Stew

2 whole chicken breasts,
    deboned, cut into 1-inch
    cubes
$1/4$ cup butter or bacon drippings
2 to 3 onions, thinly sliced
1 cup sliced celery with leaves
1 clove of garlic, minced
1 pound boneless beef chuck, cut
    into 1-inch cubes
1 pound boneless pork, cut into
    1-inch cubes
2 cups chicken stock
2 tablespoons fresh lemon juice
    or white wine
1 jalapeño, minced, or
    $1/4$ teaspoon cayenne pepper
1 tablespoon Worcestershire
    sauce

$1/4$ cup catsup
$1 1/2$ pounds tomatoes, peeled,
    seeded, or 1 large can
    tomatoes, drained
$1/2$ teaspoon marjoram
$1/2$ teaspoon thyme leaves
2 teaspoons sugar
$1 1/2$ cups fresh butter beans, or
    1 (10-ounce) package frozen
    butter beans, thawed
$1 1/2$ cups fresh corn kernels, or
    1 (10-ounce) package frozen
    corn kernels, thawed
1 cup barbecue sauce
salt to taste
pepper to taste

Sauté the chicken in the butter in a 5-quart saucepan until browned and cooked through. Remove and reserve the chicken.

Add the onions, celery and garlic to the saucepan. Sauté until tender. Add the beef and pork. Sauté until the meat is browned.

Add the chicken stock, lemon juice, jalapeño, Worcestershire sauce and catsup and mix well. Simmer, covered, for 30 minutes.

Add the tomatoes, marjoram, thyme, sugar, butter beans and corn and mix gently. Simmer, uncovered, until the stew is thickened. Add the chicken and barbecue sauce during the last 10 minutes cooking time. Season with salt and pepper.

Yield: 6 servings

Carpaccio

2 pounds frozen beef top round,
    partially thawed
fresh lemon juice
olive oil
2 to 3 tablespoons minced
    drained capers

2 to 3 tablespoons minced
    parsley
freshly ground pepper to taste
3 to 4 mushrooms, thinly sliced
    (optional)

Cut the beef into 12 to 18 thin slices. Pound the beef gently until the slices are paper thin. Arrange 2 to 3 slices of beef in the center of each of 6 serving plates.

Sprinkle the beef generously with lemon juice and brush lightly with olive oil. Combine the capers and parsley in a bowl and mix well. Place about 1 teaspoon of the mixture on each serving of beef. Season with pepper and top with mushroom slices.

Yield: 6 servings

For an elegant progressive dinner, guests began with hors d'oeuvre, including Carpaccio, at one home and were then transported by horse and carriage to the riverfront for dinner, quaffing Champagne on the way. They feasted on a gourmet picnic while listening to the symphony. They then traveled by horse and carriage to another house for dessert.

Chicken à la Lowell

4 large chicken breasts, deboned
salt and pepper to taste
Italian herbs and seasonings
    to taste

Dijon mustard to taste
4 slices mozzarella cheese
2 tablespoons olive oil
Mushroom Tomato Sauce

Pound the chicken between 2 sheets of waxed paper until thin. Remove and discard the top sheet of waxed paper. Season the chicken with salt, pepper, Italian herbs and Italian seasonings. Spread Dijon mustard over the chicken. Top each piece with 1 slice of cheese. Roll up the chicken lengthwise, pinching the ends to seal; do not use wooden picks. Chill, covered, until the chicken will remain rolled up.

Heat the olive oil in a skillet and add the chicken rolls. Sauté until browned and cooked through. Spoon the Mushroom Tomato Sauce over the chicken. Cook until heated through.

Serve the chicken over a bed of hot cooked rice. Spoon the sauce over the chicken.

Yield: 4 servings

Mushroom Tomato Sauce

1 bunch scallions, chopped
8 ounces mushrooms, chopped
3 tomatoes, peeled, chopped

olive oil
white wine

Combine the scallions, mushrooms and tomatoes in a saucepan. Stir in a small amount of olive oil. Cook until heated through. Sprinkle a small amount of white wine over the sauce. Cook for several minutes.

Yield: 2 to 3 cups

Lobster Salad

1 (1¹/₄- to 1¹/₂-pound) lobster
salt to taste
mayonnaise
grated onion to taste
minced celery to taste

Place the lobster in 2 inches of
boiling salted water in a large
saucepan. Steam, covered, for
20 minutes. Let stand until
the lobster is cool enough to
handle. Remove the meat from
the tail and claws; cut the meat
into pieces into a bowl. Stir in
enough mayonnaise to make of
the desired consistency. Stir in
the onion and celery.

Yield: 3 to 4 servings

Vitello Tonnato

4 pounds leg of veal, boned,
    butterflied
3 to 4 anchovy fillets, drained
1 tablespoon olive oil
bouquet garni (2 teaspoons bay
    leaf, 2 teaspoons thyme and
    5 sprigs of parsley)
1 cup chopped onion
¹/₂ cup sliced celery
2 cloves of garlic, crushed
1 teaspoon salt
1 cup (about) water
1 cup (about) dry white wine

Lay the veal flat. Place the anchovies on top of the veal and roll up tightly.
Secure in 3 or 4 places with kitchen string. Heat the olive oil in a skillet and
add the veal. Cook until browned on all sides.

Place the veal in a deep heavy kettle that fits the veal closely. Tie the
bouquet garni together or place in a cheesecloth bag. Add the bouquet garni,
onion, celery, garlic and salt to the kettle. Add enough water and white wine
to cover the veal. Simmer, covered, for 1¹/₄ hours or until the veal is tender.
Remove from the heat and let cool.

Drain the veal. Chill, covered, overnight. Cut the veal into thin slices.
Serve with Tuna Sauce and cherry tomatoes.

Yield: 8 to 10 servings

Tuna Sauce

1¹/₂ cups mayonnaise
1 (6-ounce) can tuna, drained
6 anchovy fillets, drained
2 tablespoons lemon juice
3 tablespoons drained capers

Process the mayonnaise, tuna, anchovies, lemon juice and half the capers in
a blender until smooth. Stir in the remaining 1¹/₂ tablespoons capers.

Yield: 2 to 2¹/₄ cups

16

Vincent Russo's Deviled Crab

¹/₂ cup chopped onion	1 tablespoon dry mustard
¹/₄ cup chopped green or red bell pepper	1 tablespoon Worcestershire sauce
¹/₄ cup chopped celery	juice of ¹/₂ lemon
¹/₄ cup butter	salt to taste
2 tablespoons flour	pepper to taste
³/₄ cup milk	1 egg, beaten
¹/₄ cup chili sauce	1 pound claw crab meat
dash of cayenne pepper	2 tablespoons chopped parsley
¹/₂ teaspoon sage	1 cup seasoned bread crumbs

Cook the onion, green pepper and celery in the butter in a saucepan until tender. Blend in the flour. Stir in the milk gradually. Cook until thickened, stirring constantly.

Add the chili sauce, cayenne pepper, sage, dry mustard, Worcestershire sauce and lemon juice and mix gently. Season with salt and pepper. Add the egg gradually, stirring constantly. Add the crab meat, parsley and bread crumbs and mix gently.

Spoon the mixture into 8 aluminum crab shells. Bake at 350 degrees until browned.

Yield: 8 servings

Picnic Crawfish Salad

1 pound cooked crawfish or
    shrimp
1 cup chopped celery
1/2 cup chopped purple onion or
    Vidalia onion
1 1/2 cups artichoke hearts, cut
    into quarters
1 cup chopped mixed red and
    yellow bell peppers
1/4 cup drained capers
1/2 cup pitted kalamata olives

1/2 cup (about) chopped Italian
    parsley
1 tablespoon grated lemon zest
salt and pepper to taste
1/2 cup white balsamic vinegar
dash of Tabasco sauce
juice of 1 lemon
1/4 teaspoon cracked pepper
1 teaspoon kosher salt
1 cup extra-virgin olive oil
baby salad greens

For the salad, combine the crawfish, celery, onion, artichoke hearts, bell peppers, capers, olives, parsley, lemon zest and salt and pepper to taste in a large bowl and mix well.

For the dressing, whisk the vinegar, Tabasco sauce, lemon juice, 1/4 teaspoon pepper and 1 teaspoon kosher salt in a medium bowl until mixed. Add the olive oil gradually, whisking until the mixture is thick.

Add the dressing to the salad and mix gently. Adjust the seasonings. Chill, covered, until serving time.

Serve on a bed of baby salad greens. Garnish with yellow and red tomatoes and avocado slices.

Yield: 4 to 6 servings

from Julia Cohen of The Preferred Caterers

Orzo and Crab Salad with Lime Dressing

2 cups orzo
1 pound cooked snow crab meat
    or blue crab meat
$1/2$ cup chopped fresh cilantro or
    parsley

$1/2$ cup chopped green onions
Lime Dressing
1 bunch watercress

Cook the orzo using the package directions. Rinse with cold water and drain well. Place the orzo in a large bowl. Add the crab meat, cilantro and green onions and mix gently. Add the Lime Dressing and toss gently. Spoon onto a large platter and surround with watercress.

Yield: 8 to 10 servings

Lime Dressing

2 jalapeños, minced
1 clove of garlic, minced
$1/2$ teaspoon salt
$1/2$ teaspoon pepper
$1/3$ cup lime juice

2 tablespoons honey
$1^1/2$ tablespoons Thai fish sauce
    or soy sauce
1 tablespoon olive oil
1 tablespoon sesame oil

Combine the jalapeños, garlic, salt, pepper, lime juice, honey, fish sauce, olive oil and sesame oil in a bowl and whisk until mixed.

Yield: $3/4$ to 1 cup

Spicy Thai Beef Salad

1 (8-ounce) beef tenderloin
baby romaine lettuce, chopped
1 red onion, chopped
1 cucumber, chopped

1 plum tomato, chopped
garlic croutons to taste
Spicy Vinaigrette

Grill the tenderloin to the desired degree of doneness; then slice into strips. Combine the tenderloin strips, lettuce, onion, cucumber, tomato and croutons in a salad bowl and toss lightly. Add the Spicy Vinaigrette and toss until mixed.

Yield: 2 servings

Spicy Vinaigrette

1 ounce jalapeños, chopped
2 tablespoons sesame oil
¼ cup soy sauce
¼ teaspoon cayenne pepper
2 teaspoons garlic powder

2 teaspoons chopped fresh
   cilantro
¼ cup olive oil
salt to taste
pepper to taste

Combine the jalapeños, sesame oil, soy sauce, cayenne pepper, garlic powder, cilantro and olive oil in a blender container and process until mixed. Season with salt and pepper.

Yield: ³/4 to 1 cup

from Chef W. Scott Grimmitt of Season's Restaurant

Chutney and Walnut Chicken Salad

2 1/2 pounds chicken breasts
1/2 cup mayonnaise or low-fat
    mayonnaise
1/2 cup sour cream or low-fat sour
    cream
1/2 cup chopped mango chutney

3/4 cup chopped walnuts
1 small red or green bell pepper,
    chopped
salt to taste
freshly ground pepper to taste

Simmer the chicken in water to cover in a saucepan or cook in a pressure cooker until the chicken is cooked through; drain well. Remove and discard the skin and bones. Cut the chicken into 1-inch pieces. Mix the mayonnaise, sour cream and chutney in a bowl. Stir in the chicken, walnuts and bell pepper. Season with salt and pepper. Serve on a bed of lettuce or use as a sandwich spread with rye bread.

Yield: 4 servings

Sweet-and-Sour Spinach Salad

3 tablespoons rice wine vinegar
3 tablespoons Chinese plum
    sauce
1 teaspoon vegetable oil
1/2 teaspoon crushed red pepper

3 cups tightly packed torn
    spinach leaves
1 1/2 cups sliced mushrooms
1 hard-cooked egg, chopped
1/2 teaspoon toasted sesame seeds

Combine the vinegar, plum sauce, oil and red pepper in a jar with a tight-fitting lid. Shake well to mix and set aside. Toss the spinach, mushrooms and egg in a bowl. Add the dressing and toss again. Sprinkle with the sesame seeds and toss very gently. Serve immediately.

Yield: 4 servings

White Bean and Shrimp Salad

1 cup navy beans	1 cup sliced fennel bulbs
4 cups water	1 teaspoon salt
2 sprigs of fresh thyme	freshly ground pepper to taste
1 bay leaf	Tarragon Vinaigrette
1 clove of garlic	romaine or Bibb lettuce
1 pound shrimp, cooked, peeled	chopped chives to taste

Rinse and sort the beans and soak in water to cover overnight; drain well. Combine the beans, 4 cups water, thyme, bay leaf and garlic in a medium saucepan. Bring to a boil and reduce the heat. Simmer for 45 minutes or until the beans are tender but not mushy; drain well. Remove and discard the bay leaf and garlic.

Combine the beans, shrimp, fennel, salt and pepper in a medium bowl and toss gently. Add the Tarragon Vinaigrette and toss again.

Arrange the lettuce on individual plates. Divide the salad evenly among the plates. Sprinkle with chives.

Yield: 4 servings

Tarragon Vinaigrette

4 teaspoons white wine vinegar	4 teaspoons olive oil
2 tablespoons chopped fresh tarragon	salt to taste
	pepper to taste

Combine the vinegar, tarragon and olive oil in a bowl and whisk until mixed. Season with salt and pepper.

Yield: 1/4 to 1/2 cup

Savannah Brittle Bread

This once-secret recipe is from Colonial times in Savannah.

2³/₄ cups (about) flour
¹/₄ cup sugar
¹/₂ teaspoon salt
¹/₂ teaspoon baking powder

¹/₂ cup butter
1 cup plain yogurt
salt to taste

Mix the flour, sugar, ¹/₂ teaspoon salt and baking powder in a bowl. Cut in the butter until crumbly. Stir in the yogurt, mixing until a soft dough forms and adding additional flour if the dough is too sticky. Dust lightly with additional flour. Chill, covered, overnight.

Divide the dough into walnut-sized pieces and roll each piece into a ball. Roll each ball into a very thin 5- to 6-inch round on a floured surface. Place on nonstick baking sheets. Sprinkle generously with salt to taste. Bake 1 sheet at a time at 425 degrees for 5 to 8 minutes or until puffed and lightly browned.

After all the bread is baked, turn off the oven and let cool slightly. Pile all the bread onto 1 baking sheet and return to the warm oven. Let stand overnight. This bread will keep in a plastic bag in the refrigerator or freezer for up to 1 month.

Yield: 2¹/₂ to 3 dozen

Chocolate Chip Muffins

2 cups sugar
1¹/₂ cups vegetable oil
5 eggs
1 teaspoon vanilla extract
4 to 5 large bananas, chopped
3 cups flour
1 teaspoon baking soda
1 teaspoon baking powder
1 teaspoon salt
¹/₂ teaspoon cinnamon
2 cups toasted pecan pieces
1 to 2 cups chocolate chips

Mix the sugar, oil, eggs, vanilla and bananas in a mixer bowl. Add the flour, baking soda, baking powder, salt and cinnamon and beat until mixed. Stir in the pecans and chocolate chips. Fill nonstick muffin cups ¹/₂ full with batter. Bake at 350 degrees for 12 to 17 minutes or until the muffins test done. For a lower-fat version of these muffins, substitute ¹/₂ cup vegetable oil and 1 cup low-fat sour cream for the 1¹/₂ cups vegetable oil.

Yield: 1 to 2 dozen

23

Blueberry Pineapple Crisp

3 cups (about) blueberries
1 (20-ounce) can crushed
    pineapple
²/₃ cup packed light brown sugar
¹/₂ cup flour

¹/₂ cup quick-cooking oats
¹/₂ teaspoon cinnamon
¹/₂ teaspoon mace
¹/₃ cup melted margarine

Spread the blueberries in a greased 9x13-inch casserole. Spoon the undrained pineapple over the blueberries. Mix the brown sugar, flour, oats, cinnamon and mace in a bowl. Sprinkle over the fruit. Spoon the margarine over the top. Bake at 350 degrees for 35 minutes or until bubbly.

Yield: 8 servings

Chocolate Espresso Cookies

3 ounces bittersweet chocolate,
    chopped
1 cup chocolate chips
¹/₂ cup unsalted butter, cut into
    pieces
3 eggs
1 cup plus 2 tablespoons sugar

2¹/₄ teaspoons finely ground
    coffee beans
³/₄ cup flour
¹/₃ teaspoon baking powder
¹/₄ teaspoon salt
1 cup chocolate chips
1 cup chopped walnuts

Melt the bittersweet chocolate, 1 cup chocolate chips and butter in a heavy saucepan, stirring constantly until smooth; set aside. Beat the eggs, sugar and ground coffee at high speed in a mixer bowl for 3 minutes or until thick and pale yellow. Beat in the chocolate mixture gradually. Combine the flour, baking powder and salt in a bowl. Sift into the batter, beating just until mixed. Stir in 1 cup chocolate chips and walnuts. Drop by tablespoonfuls 2 inches apart onto greased or parchment-lined cookie sheets. Bake at 350 degrees for 8 to 10 minutes or until puffed and cracked on top.

Yield: 3 to 3¹/₂ dozen

Pecan Pralines

1 cup packed light or dark brown
  sugar
1 cup sugar

¹/₂ cup water
2 tablespoons margarine
1 cup chopped pecans

Combine the brown sugar, sugar and water in a microwave-safe bowl, stirring until the sugar is dissolved. Microwave on High for 6 minutes, stirring once. Microwave for 2 minutes longer. Stir in the margarine and pecans, beating until the mixture begins to thicken. Drop by spoonfuls onto waxed paper.

Yield: 2 to 2¹/₂ dozen

Chocolate Caramel Layered Squares

1 (14-ounce) package caramels
¹/₃ cup evaporated milk
1 (2-layer) package German
  chocolate cake mix

¹/₃ cup evaporated milk
³/₄ cup margarine, softened
1 cup chopped pecans or walnuts
1 cup semisweet chocolate chips

Combine the caramels and ¹/₃ cup evaporated milk in a double boiler. Cook until the caramels are melted, stirring constantly. Remove from the heat. Combine the cake mix, ¹/₃ cup evaporated milk and margarine in a mixer bowl and beat until a soft dough forms. Stir in the pecans. Press half the cake mix mixture into a greased 9x13-inch baking pan. Bake at 350 degrees for 6 minutes. Sprinkle evenly with the chocolate chips. Spoon the caramel mixture over the top. Crumble the remaining cake mix mixture over the top. Bake for 15 to 18 minutes or until a wooden pick inserted near the center comes out clean. Let cool and cut into small squares.

Yield: 5 dozen

Chamber Concerts...
Maestro's Favorites

Before attending a Friday evening concert by the chamber orchestra at the
Telfair Academy, close friends may get together to enjoy a fine dinner and good
conversation at one of Savannah's popular restaurants. Every maitre d' knows
that prompt service is a requisite for a pre-concert dinner, and every chef can
expect light fare to be the order of the evening.

Not everyone who applauds Maestro Philip Greenberg as he mounts the
podium that evening will be aware that his culinary skills run a close second to
his musical knowledge. The Maestro can be counted on by the members of the
Guild to don his apron and chef's cap to prepare an innovative medley of
delights for a PARTIES A LA CARTE dinner. Does osso buco prepared
with sherry, cognac, and marsala sound appealing as a main course?
The Maestro's coffee flan with Kahlúa caramel sauce will do nicely for
dessert. Perhaps the orchestra's concertmaster will arrive at the
party to thrill the guests with a Bach violin sonata.

Contents

Menu

The Maestro's International Dinner

Smoked Salmon Mousse with Citrus Vodka (page 30)

Stuffed Grape Leaves (page 120)

Herbed potatoes

Cold Barbecued Salmon with Mustard Dill Crust (page 31)

Salad of mixed greens

French onion soup

Osso Buco with Sherry, Cognac and Marsala (page 32)

Grilled Portobella Mushrooms (page 32)

Sweet Potatoes with Cointreau (page 165)

White Chocolate Mousse with Raspberries in Bittersweet Chocolate Cups (page 33)

Coffee Flan with Kahlúa Sauce (page 34)

Smoked Salmon Mousse with Citrus Vodka

8 ounces smoked salmon
8 ounces cream cheese, softened
1/3 cup chopped scallions
1/4 cup finely chopped dillweed
juice of 1 lemon

freshly ground pepper to taste
1/8 teaspoon cumin (optional)
Tabasco sauce to taste
2 tablespoons lemon vodka or
    plain vodka

Combine the salmon, cream cheese, scallions, dillweed, lemon juice, pepper, cumin, Tabasco sauce and vodka in a food processor container. Process until finely puréed. Spoon into a serving dish and smooth the top. Cover and chill thoroughly.

To serve, let stand until cool. Serve with buttered toast. Serve chopped onion and drained capers on the side.

Yield: 6 to 8 servings

Cold Barbecued Salmon with Mustard Dill Crust

¹/₂ large salmon fillet
salt and pepper to taste
4 to 8 ounces whole yellow
    mustard seeds

2 to 3 bunches dillweed with
    stems

Rinse the salmon and pat dry. Season with salt and pepper. Place the mustard seeds in a shallow dish. Press the fleshy side of the salmon into the mustard seeds until coated. Remove the salmon from the dish and press mustard seeds into any remaining bare spots. Cover generously with the dillweed. Place the salmon between 2 baking racks or wire cooling racks. If racks are not available, tie the salmon with thin wire. Do not secure with string; the string will burn off.

Place the salmon skin side down on the grill 3 to 4 inches above the heat source. Grill for 8 to 10 minutes or until the skin becomes dry and cracked and somewhat burned. Turn the salmon over. Grill for 5 to 8 minutes or until cooked to taste. Serve with your favorite creamy dill sauce. The salmon may be broiled instead of grilled.

Editor's Note: The dill will burn and smoke the salmon, but be careful not to overcook or the mustard seeds will burn and become bitter. This can best be accomplished by cooking the salmon longer on the skin side; this will also allow the skin to be removed more easily when serving.

Yield: 2 servings

Grilled Portobella Mushrooms

1/4 cup butter
5 to 6 shallots, minced
8 to 10 ounces (about) dry
   white wine
8 to 10 ounces (about)
   beef broth
4 large portobella
   mushrooms, cut into
   1/2-inch slices
2 tablespoons minced garlic
salt and pepper to taste

Melt the butter in a skillet. Add the shallots. Sauté until translucent. Add the wine, beef broth and mushrooms and mix well. Sauté for 10 to 20 minutes or until the mushrooms are tender and of a uniform color. Add the garlic during the last 2 to 3 minutes cooking time. Season with salt and pepper. If more liquid is needed when sautéing the mushrooms, add equal amounts of wine and beef broth.

Yield: 4 servings

Osso Buco with Sherry, Cognac and Marsala

8 veal shanks
salt to taste
pepper to taste
1/2 cup flour
2 tablespoons olive oil
1/4 cup butter
10 to 15 baby carrots
1 large carrot, chopped
1 cup chopped onion
6 cloves of garlic, minced
1 medium bay leaf
2 tablespoons chopped parsley
3 1/2 cups chopped tomatoes
1 cup consommé
1 cup chicken broth
1/2 cup Cognac
1/2 cup sweet marsala
3/4 cup cream sherry
3 small pieces lemon peel
3 small pieces orange peel
1/2 cup whipping cream
1/4 cup sweet marsala

Season the veal with salt and pepper and coat with the flour. Heat the olive oil and butter in a large skillet and add the veal. Sauté until browned on each side. Remove the veal to a large baking dish and keep warm. Add the baby carrots, large carrot, onion and garlic to the skillet. Cook until the onion begins to brown. Remove from the heat. Add the bay leaf, parsley and tomatoes. Mix well and return to the heat. Cook for 5 minutes. Add the consommé, chicken broth, Cognac, 1/2 cup marsala, sherry, lemon peel and orange peel and mix well. Adjust the seasonings and remove and discard the bay leaf. Spoon the mixture over the veal.

Bake, covered, at 350 degrees for 1 1/2 to 2 hours or until the veal is cooked through. Remove the veal to a serving platter and keep warm. Remove 1/2 cup of the cooking liquid from the baking dish to a small bowl. Add the whipping cream, stirring until the mixture has cooled slightly. Add the mixture to the remaining cooking liquid in the baking dish and mix well. Stir in 1/4 cup marsala. Serve the gravy with the veal.

Editor's Note: If the gravy is too thick, thin it with a mixture of equal amounts of cornstarch and cold water.

Yield: 8 servings

White Chocolate Mousse with Raspberries in Bittersweet Chocolate Cups

To prepare the chocolate cups, you will need 12 small round balloons. Water bomb balloons, available at party supply stores, work best.

8 ounces white chocolate
2 cups whipping cream

16 ounces bittersweet chocolate
2 cups fresh raspberries

For the mousse, melt the white chocolate in a double boiler over hot water, stirring constantly. Bring the whipping cream to a boil in a saucepan. Boil for 30 seconds. Whisk the hot cream into the white chocolate until blended and smooth. Chill, covered, overnight, stirring once after several hours. Beat the white chocolate mixture at high speed in a large mixer bowl for 4 to 6 minutes or until stiff; do not overbeat. Cover and chill thoroughly.

For the chocolate cups, melt the bittersweet chocolate in a double boiler, stirring constantly. Cool for 5 minutes. Blow up the balloons to a 3- to 4-inch diameter. Dip the bottom half of a balloon into the melted chocolate at a 45-degree angle; then dip the opposite side of the bottom half into the chocolate. Turn the balloon to the 2 empty sides and repeat. You now have a "tulip" with 4 "petals." Set on a baking sheet covered with plastic wrap or waxed paper. Repeat with the remaining balloons and melted chocolate. Chill in the refrigerator for 15 minutes or in the freezer for 5 minutes or until set. Hold the top half of 1 balloon and pop with a pin; peel the balloon away gently. Repeat with the remaining balloons. If the bottom of a balloon sticks, warm it carefully with your finger and it will release.

Purée the raspberries in a food processor. Strain the raspberries through a sieve. Spoon a shallow pool of raspberry purée onto each dessert plate to hold each chocolate cup. Set each cup gently on the raspberry purée and fill the cups with the chilled mousse.

Yield: 12 servings

Coffee Flan with Kahlúa Sauce

1 cup sugar
1/4 cup water
2 cups milk
1 cup whipping cream
1 cup half-and-half

4 teaspoons instant coffee powder
3 eggs
3 egg yolks
1/3 cup sugar
2 tablespoons Kahlúa

Place six 1/2-cup ramekins in a large baking pan. Heat in a 325-degree oven for 10 minutes or until the ramekins are hot.

Bring 1 cup sugar and water to a boil in a small heavy saucepan, stirring until the sugar dissolves. Boil without stirring for 6 minutes or until the mixture is golden brown. Spoon the mixture into the hot ramekins immediately, tilting carefully to coat the side of the ramekins. Let cool.

Bring the milk, whipping cream and half-and-half to a boil in a large heavy saucepan. Remove from the heat and stir in the coffee powder. Whisk the eggs, egg yolks and 1/3 cup sugar in a large bowl. Stir a small amount of the hot cream mixture into the egg mixture; stir the egg mixture into the hot cream mixture. Stir in the Kahlúa.

Divide the custard evenly among the prepared ramekins. Return the ramekins to the large baking pan. Add enough boiling water to the baking pan to reach halfway up the side of the ramekins. Bake at 325 degrees for 1 1/4 hours or until the edges are set and the centers move only slightly when gently shaken. Remove the ramekins from the water. Chill for 6 hours or until the custard is set. Loosen the edge of the custard from the ramekin with a sharp knife. Invert onto dessert plates to serve.

Yield: 6 servings

Philip's Marinated Beef Tenderloin

1 whole beef tenderloin, trimmed
2 tablespoons olive oil
1 bottle Reunite Lambrusco wine
2 tablespoons dark brown sugar

$^1/_4$ cup soy sauce
1 tablespoon Maggi seasoning
   sauce (meat glaze)

Score the beef in a cross-hatch fashion with a fork and rub with the olive oil. Combine the wine, brown sugar, soy sauce and seasoning sauce in a bowl, stirring until the brown sugar is dissolved. Place the beef in a baking dish or roasting bag and add the wine mixture. Marinate in the refrigerator for 1 to 2 days. Remove the beef from the marinade, discarding the remaining marinade.

Sear the beef in a skillet or on a grill. Place the seared beef in a baking pan. Bake, covered tightly with foil, at 400 to 425 degrees for 30 to 40 minutes or until a meat thermometer inserted at the thickest point registers 140 degrees for rare.

Yield: 4 to 6 servings

Chinese Lacquered Duck with Coffee Mandarin Glaze

2 (5-pound) ducks
4 cups kosher salt
1 gallon water

2 cups honey
Coffee Mandarin Glaze

Rub the ducks thoroughly with the salt. Place the ducks on a rack in a shallow pan. Chill, uncovered, for up to 24 hours. Rinse the ducks under cold running water to remove all the salt. Trim away and discard any excess fat. Bring the water to a boil in a stockpot over high heat. Stir in the honey. Immerse 1 of the ducks in the honey mixture for 4 minutes. Remove the duck carefully and drain well. Repeat the procedure with the second duck. Place the ducks on a wire rack in a roasting pan. Bake at 450 degrees for 30 minutes. Reduce the oven temperature to 300 degrees. Roast for 1 hour or until the skin resembles black lacquer. To carve, remove the breasts and legs from the ducks, leaving the skin intact. Slice the leg meat from the bone and place on warm plates. Slice the breast meat crosswise and fan the slices on the plates. Drizzle with Coffee Mandarin Glaze.

Yield: 4 servings

Coffee Mandarin Glaze

¼ cup sugar
2 tablespoons unsalted butter
½ cup fresh orange juice

½ cup strong black coffee
¼ cup coffee liqueur
1 teaspoon arrowroot

Cook the sugar in a heavy medium nonreactive saucepan over medium heat until light brown, stirring constantly. Add the butter, stirring until melted. Stir in the orange juice, coffee and liqueur. Simmer until the sugar is completely dissolved. Stir in the arrowroot. Simmer for 3 minutes or until thickened. Remove from the heat and keep warm.

Yield: 1½ to 1¾ cups

Philip's Tiramisù

²/₃ cup sugar
¹/₄ cup water
4 large egg yolks
¹/₂ teaspoon vanilla extract
9 ounces mascarpone cheese,
    softened
4 to 6 tablespoons dark rum

4 to 6 tablespoons amaretto
1 cup whipping cream, whipped
12 biscotti di Savoiardi (Italian
    ladyfingers)
¹/₃ cup espresso
3 ounces dark sweet chocolate,
    grated

Combine the sugar and water in a small saucepan. Bring to a boil over medium heat, stirring constantly. Boil until just before the mixture registers 225 degrees on a candy thermometer, brushing the side of the saucepan with cold water to prevent the syrup from boiling over. Set aside.

Beat the egg yolks in a mixer bowl. Add the syrup in a stream, beating constantly until very thick and pale yellow. Beat in the vanilla.

Whisk the mascarpone cheese, rum and amaretto in a bowl until blended and smooth. Add the egg mixture and mix gently. Fold in the whipped cream.

Line the edges of a 6-cup serving dish with biscotti. Drizzle the espresso over the biscotti. Spoon the mascarpone mixture into the dish, smoothing the top. Chill, covered with plastic wrap, for 3 hours to overnight. Sprinkle with the grated chocolate at serving time.

Editor's Note: If the tiramisù does not set up properly during chilling, place it in the freezer for about 30 minutes before serving. Use only biscotti di Savoiardi in this recipe, not other ladyfingers.

Yield: 6 servings

Lemon Curd

1/2 cup sugar
2 eggs
2 egg yolks
1/2 cup strained fresh
    lemon juice
2 teaspoons grated
    lemon peel
6 tablespoons unsalted
    butter, cut into small
    pieces

Whisk the sugar, eggs and egg yolks in a medium saucepan. Add the lemon juice and lemon peel and mix well. Add the butter. Cook over medium heat just until the mixture begins to bubble, whisking constantly; do not boil. Spoon the mixture into a bowl and press plastic wrap directly onto the surface. Chill thoroughly. Serve with scones or fresh fruit. Lemon Curd will keep for up to 3 days in the refrigerator.

Yield: 2 cups

Never-Fail Scones

6 cups flour
3/4 cup sugar
1/3 cup baking powder
1 cup plus 2 teaspoons unsalted
    butter, cut into small pieces

2 cups buttermilk
1 1/4 cups currants or raisins
1 egg yolk, beaten (optional)
slivered almonds (optional)

Mix the flour, sugar and baking powder in a large bowl. Cut in the butter until crumbly. Add the buttermilk, mixing just until a sticky dough forms. Place the dough on a floured board and gently knead in the currants. Divide the dough into 4 equal portions. Roll each portion into 8 wedges.

Place the wedges 1/2 inch apart on nonstick baking sheets. Brush with the egg yolk; sprinkle with almonds. Bake at 350 degrees for 17 minutes or until golden brown. Serve with Lemon Curd and/or Clotted Cream.

Yield: 32 scones

Clotted Cream

1/2 cup whipping cream
2 tablespoons confectioners'
    sugar

1/2 cup sour cream

Beat the whipping cream in a mixer bowl until stiff peaks form. Add the confectioners' sugar and beat until smooth. Fold in the sour cream. Chill, covered, overnight.

Yield: 1 1/2 cups

Lapsang Souchong Poached Chicken Salad

3 pounds boneless chicken breast
3 quarts (about) water
¹/₄ cup Lapsang Souchong or
    orange pekoe tea
¹/₄ cup soy sauce
1 ounce gingerroot, chopped
1 large apple, chopped
2 cloves of garlic, chopped

2 tablespoons chopped red bell
    pepper
2 tablespoons chopped yellow
    bell pepper
2 cups mayonnaise
¹/₂ teaspoon salt, or to taste
¹/₈ teaspoon white pepper, or
    to taste

Trim any fat from the chicken; cut the chicken into halves. Combine the chicken and enough water to cover in a 5-quart saucepan. Add the tea and soy sauce. Bring to a boil; reduce the heat to just below the boiling point. Poach for 30 minutes or until the chicken is cooked through. Let stand to cool. Drain and rinse the chicken and cut into medium chunks.

Combine the gingerroot, apple, garlic, red pepper and yellow pepper in a bowl. Add the mayonnaise and mix well. Stir in the chicken. Season with salt and white pepper. Serve on toasted wheat bread.

Yield: 10 servings

from Chef André Baxter of the Tea Room Restaurant

Ginger Pecan Cream Cheese

1 (2-ounce) package
   crystallized ginger
1 cup pecan pieces
32 ounces cream cheese, cut
   into $1/2$-inch chunks
thinly sliced white bread

Chop all ingredients in a food
processor in the order given,
processing in short bursts.
Spread on the bread. Trim
off the crusts and cut the bread
into attractive shapes. To serve
as tea sandwiches, top each
with another slice of bread.
For hors d'oeuvre, serve
open-faced.

Yield: 150 servings

Savannah Tomato Sandwiches

This was a secret recipe made by Savannah's most exclusive caterer during the years following the war—World War II, that is, not that "recent unpleasantness" (the War Between the States).

12 ($2^1/2$-inch) very ripe summer
   tomatoes, peeled
3 loaves thinly sliced white bread
1 loaf thinly sliced whole wheat
   bread
1 egg

2 cups mayonnaise
2 teaspoons lemon juice
dash of cayenne pepper
1 tablespoon grated onion
$1/2$ cup extra-virgin olive oil
seasoned salt

Chill the tomatoes for 12 to 24 hours. Slice the tomatoes and place on paper towels to drain. Cut $2^1/2$-inch rounds from each slice of bread, discarding the bread scraps or reserving for another use. Use a tiny cookie cutter or biscuit cutter to cut some very small holes in all the whole wheat bread rounds and $1/3$ of the white bread rounds. Cover with damp towels.

Cook the egg in simmering water in a saucepan for 1 minute or until coddled. Mix the coddled egg, mayonnaise, lemon juice, cayenne and onion in a bowl. Whisk in the olive oil in a steady stream.

Spread mayonnaise mixture on each solid bread round and top with a tomato slice. Sprinkle with seasoned salt. Top with a bread round with holes.

Yield: 40 sandwiches

Poppy Seed Tea Bread

2 cups flour
1 cup sugar
¹/₄ cup poppy seeds
1¹/₂ teaspoons baking powder
¹/₄ teaspoon baking soda
¹/₂ teaspoon salt

³/₄ cup buttermilk
2 eggs, beaten
¹/₂ cup melted unsalted butter,
  cooled
1¹/₂ teaspoons vanilla extract
Chocolate Glaze (optional)

Mix the flour, sugar, poppy seeds, baking powder, baking soda and salt in a large bowl and make a well in the center. Mix the buttermilk, eggs, melted butter and vanilla in a medium bowl. Add to the dry ingredients, stirring just until mixed. Spoon into a greased 4x8-inch loaf pan. Bake at 350 degrees for 45 to 55 minutes or until the loaf tests done. Top with Chocolate Glaze if desired. This bread freezes well.

Yield: 10 to 14 servings

Black-Eyed Susans

1 (16-ounce) package whole
  pitted dates
small pecans
1 pound Cheddar cheese,
  shredded

1 cup melted butter
3 cups flour
¹/₂ cup (about) sugar
¹/₈ teaspoon salt

Stuff each date with a pecan and set aside. Mix the cheese, melted butter, flour, sugar and salt in a bowl. Chill, covered, until firm. Wrap each date with a small piece of chilled dough and place on an ungreased cookie sheet. Bake at 325 degrees for 25 minutes or until golden brown. These cookies may be frozen before baking, but the baking time may need to be increased by about 10 minutes.

Yield: 4 dozen

Chocolate Glaze

3 ounces unsweetened
  chocolate
¹/₄ cup butter
3 cups confectioners' sugar
1 teaspoon vanilla extract
¹/₄ cup (about) boiling water

Heat the chocolate and butter in a saucepan until melted, stirring constantly. Remove from the heat. Stir in the confectioners' sugar and vanilla. Stir in boiling water 1 teaspoon at a time until of a glaze consistency.

Yield: 3 cups

Lemon Squares

2 cups flour
1/2 cup confectioners' sugar
1 cup butter
4 eggs, beaten
2 cups sugar

1/3 cup lemon juice
1/4 cup flour
1/2 teaspoon salt
2 teaspoons baking powder

Sift 2 cups flour and confectioners' sugar into a bowl. Cut in the butter until crumbly. Press onto the bottom of a nonstick 9x13-inch baking pan. Bake at 350 degrees for 20 to 25 minutes or until lightly browned.

Beat the eggs, sugar and lemon juice in a bowl. Sift 1/4 cup flour, salt and baking powder together and stir into the egg mixture. Spoon over the baked crust. Bake at 350 degrees for 25 minutes. Let cool and cut into squares.

Yield: 18 to 24 servings

from caterer Susan Mason

Danish Short Cookies

2 cups flour
3/4 cup butter
3/4 cup confectioners' sugar

2 egg yolks
1 teaspoon vanilla extract

Combine the flour, butter, confectioners' sugar, egg yolks and vanilla in a bowl and mix well. Chill, covered, for 1 hour. Roll on a floured surface and cut into desired shapes. Place on a nonstick cookie sheet. Bake at 375 degrees for 10 to 12 minutes or until lightly browned. Cool on a wire rack. If desired, cooled cookies may be dipped halfway into melted chocolate chips and then cooled on a wire rack in the refrigerator for several minutes while the chocolate sets. Store in an airtight container.

Yield: 2 dozen

Chocolate Creams

1 cup melted butter
2 pounds confectioners' sugar
1 (5-ounce) can sweetened
   condensed milk

1 pound (about) chocolate
vegetable oil

Combine the melted butter and confectioners' sugar in a large bowl and mix well. Add the condensed milk and mix well. Spread ¾ inch thick on a baking sheet, leaving a margin around each side. Chill until firm. Cut into ¾-inch squares. Chill until firm. Shape the squares into balls. Chill until firm enough to dip.

Melt the chocolate slowly in a double boiler, stirring frequently and thinning with a small amount of vegetable oil if needed. Dip each ball into the melted chocolate and lift out with a fork. Try to coat each ball completely and evenly with chocolate. Cool on a baking sheet.

Yield: 2 pounds

Brunches and All That Jazz

Of all the PARTIES A LA CARTE, the jazz brunches seem to sell out most quickly. That's because of the combinations of tastes, sights and sites, sounds of music and voices, and the purely southern atmosphere that is its most regional at jazz brunches. Mimosas, Bloody Marys, and sweet iced tea—croissants and biscuits—country ham and southern sausage—all these richly delicious foods that comprise a party meal—those are the things we revel in at morning's end.

Of course, there is music—those sad, sweet sounds echoing hints of the old-time streets called Basin, Rampart, and Bourbon that gave birth to the blues. The Preservation Hall Jazz Band from New Orleans has played for Pops concerts, and the Tom Turpin Jazz Fest is held annually. Even when the players change, the rhythm and soul continue in our minds and hearts. Nostalgia flavors jazz brunches just as much as the rich food. Slowly revolving ceiling fans move languid air, and laughter lingers into lazy afternoons.

Contents

Menu

Laissez les Bons Temps Roulez

Cajun Barbecued Shrimp
(page 48)

Oyster and Artichoke Soup
(page 49)

Creole salad

Trout Marguery (page 50)

Chicken Etouffée (page 51)

Cajun Red Beans and Rice
with Sausage
(page 57)

Maque Choux (page 50)

French bread

Bread Pudding with
Whiskey Sauce
(page 52)

Avocados and Shrimp

24 small shrimp, cooked
2 tablespoons sliced scallions
1 egg
1/4 cup wine vinegar
2 tablespoons Dijon mustard
1/2 cup olive oil
2 large avocados
lemon juice
2 tablespoons minced parsley

Place the shrimp and scallions in a serving dish. Cook the egg in simmering water in a saucepan for 1 minute or until coddled. Mix the coddled egg, vinegar and Dijon mustard in a blender container. Add the olive oil gradually with the blender running. Pour over the shrimp and scallions. Chill, covered, until serving time. Cut avocados into bite-size pieces and sprinkle with lemon juice. Stir into the shrimp mixture. Sprinkle with the parsley.

Yield: 12 servings

Cajun Barbecued Shrimp

8 pounds large shrimp with
  heads on
3 cups margarine
1 cup butter
4 teaspoons garlic flakes
1 (2-ounce) jar Lawry's seasoned
  pepper, or to taste
1 tablespoon crushed red pepper

2 pinches of oregano
5 dashes of tarragon vinegar
1 teaspoon onion flakes
1 cup dry white wine
1 teaspoon dried rosemary
4 teaspoons Worcestershire sauce
juice of 1/2 lemon
salt to taste

Place the shrimp in a baking pan with 2-inch sides. Melt the margarine and butter in a large saucepan. Add the garlic flakes, seasoned pepper, red pepper, oregano, vinegar, onion flakes, wine, rosemary, Worcestershire sauce and lemon juice and mix well. Season with salt. Spoon over the shrimp. Chill, covered, overnight, stirring once or twice.

Bake at 400 degrees for 15 to 18 minutes or until the shrimp turn pink. Serve hot with French bread for dipping.

Yield: 10 to 12 servings

Oyster and Artichoke Soup

36 oysters with their liquor
1 (12-ounce) can artichoke hearts
3 onions, chopped
1/2 cup butter or margarine
3 to 4 tablespoons flour
1 bunch green onions, chopped
5 ribs celery, chopped
4 cloves of garlic, minced

1/2 green or red bell pepper,
   chopped
2/3 cup water
1 cup milk
2 tablespoons chopped parsley
1 bay leaf
1/2 teaspoon cayenne pepper
salt and white pepper to taste

Cut the oysters into quarters and set aside, reserving the liquor. Drain the artichoke hearts, reserving the liquid. Cut the artichoke hearts into quarters and set aside.

Sauté the onions in the butter in a saucepan until tender. Add the flour. Sauté until lightly browned. Add the green onions, celery, garlic and green pepper. Cook over low heat for 2 to 3 minutes or until heated through.

Whisk in the water gradually. Cook until thickened, whisking constantly. Add the reserved artichoke liquid and artichoke hearts and mix well. Simmer for 10 to 15 minutes or until the soup is heated through and the flavors have blended.

Add the oysters, reserved liquor and milk and mix well. Simmer for 15 minutes. Add the parsley, bay leaf, cayenne pepper, salt and white pepper and mix well. Simmer for 30 minutes or until the oysters are tender and the edges curl. Remove and discard the bay leaf.

Yield: 10 servings

Maque Choux

8 ears of corn
1/2 cup chopped onion
1/4 cup chopped green or red
    bell pepper
1/2 cup chopped peeled
    tomato
1 teaspoon sugar
salt, white pepper and
    crushed red pepper
    to taste
1/2 cup bacon drippings,
    butter or margarine
1/2 cup fresh or frozen baby
    lima beans

Cut the corn kernels from
the cob with a sharp knife,
scraping to release all the
liquid. Combine the corn
kernels, liquid, onion, green
pepper, tomato, sugar, salt,
white pepper, red pepper,
bacon drippings and lima
beans in a 2-quart saucepan
and mix well. Cook, covered,
over low heat for 45 minutes,
stirring occasionally.

Yield: 6 servings

Trout Marguery

1 pound shrimp, boiled, peeled,
    deveined
2 1/2 cups mixed fish stock and
    white wine
1/4 cup butter
1/4 cup flour
2 egg yolks, beaten
1 tablespoon lemon juice
1/4 teaspoon salt
1/2 cup sliced mushrooms
1/4 cup butter
Tabasco sauce and white pepper
    to taste
4 speckled trout fillets or
    mountain trout fillets
salt and black pepper to taste
corn flour (see Editor's Note)
1/2 cup vegetable oil

Set aside 16 of the nicest shrimp for a garnish. Heat the wine mixture in a
small saucepan. Melt 1/4 cup butter in a heavy skillet and whisk in the flour.
Cook over medium-high heat until lightly browned, whisking constantly.
Reduce the heat.

Add the heated wine mixture to the skillet. Cook until thickened,
whisking constantly. Whisk in a mixture of the egg yolks and lemon juice.
Add 1/4 teaspoon salt, remaining shrimp, mushrooms, 1/4 cup butter, Tabasco
sauce and white pepper and mix well. Cook until heated through.

Season the trout with salt and black pepper to taste. Coat with corn
flour. Heat the oil in a heavy skillet until very hot. Add the trout. Pan-fry
quickly. Drain the trout on paper towels.

Arrange the trout on serving plates. Top with the wine sauce and garnish
with the reserved shrimp.

Editor's Note: If corn flour is not available, use equal parts flour and
cornmeal.

Yield: 4 servings

Chicken Étouffée

1 (4-pound) chicken
1/4 cup chopped celery
1/4 cup chopped onion
1 bay leaf
1 1/2 teaspoons salt
1 1/2 teaspoons cayenne pepper
3/4 teaspoon black pepper
1/2 teaspoon white pepper
1/2 cup bacon drippings or
   vegetable oil

3/4 cup flour
1/4 cup chopped celery
1/4 cup chopped onion
1/4 cup chopped green or red bell
   pepper
1/2 teaspoon granulated garlic
3/4 cup chopped green onions
hot cooked rice

Combine the chicken with water to cover in a stockpot. Add 1/4 cup celery,
1/4 cup onion, bay leaf, salt, cayenne pepper, black pepper and white pepper.
Cook for 1 1/2 to 2 hours or until the chicken is tender and cooked through.
Remove and discard the chicken skin and bones. Chop the chicken into
1-inch pieces. Measure out 4 cups chicken, reserving the remainder for
another use. Strain the stock through a sieve. Measure out 3 1/2 cups,
reserving the remainder for another use.

Heat the bacon drippings to the smoking point in a 9-inch cast-iron
skillet. Add the flour, whisking constantly until the roux is almost the color
of milk chocolate; do not burn. Add 1/4 cup celery, 1/4 cup onion and bell
pepper. Sauté until the vegetables are tender.

Bring the 3 1/2 cups stock to a boil in a 2-quart saucepan. Whisk in the
roux. Cook over low heat until thickened, whisking constantly. Add the
4 cups chicken, garlic and green onions and mix well. Serve over rice.

Yield: 6 servings

Bread Pudding with Whiskey Sauce

This recipe has been adapted from a very old Creole recipe.

1 large loaf dry French bread,
   torn into large pieces
1 quart milk
3 eggs, beaten
2 cups sugar

2 tablespoons vanilla extract
1 cup raisins
1/4 cup margarine
Whiskey Sauce

Combine the bread pieces with the milk in a large bowl and soak for 10 minutes. Add the eggs, sugar, vanilla and raisins and mix well.

Melt the margarine in a baking dish in a 350-degree oven. Spoon the bread mixture into the baking dish and mix well. Bake at 350 degrees for 1 hour or until very firm. Let cool and cut into 2x3-inch pieces. Place the pudding pieces in individual dessert dishes and spoon Whiskey Sauce over the top. Heat under the broiler.

Yield: 20 servings

Whiskey Sauce

1/2 cup margarine
1 cup sugar

1 egg, beaten
2 tablespoons bourbon

Combine the margarine and sugar in a 1-quart saucepan. Cook until heated through, stirring until the sugar is dissolved. Stir a small amount of the hot mixture into the egg; stir the egg into the hot mixture. Let stand until cool. Stir in the whiskey.

Yield: 1 1/2 to 2 cups

Conch Fritters

2 tablespoons unsalted butter
1/3 cup minced onion
1/4 cup minced green or red bell
    pepper
1/4 cup minced celery
1 1/2 cups flour
1 1/2 teaspoons baking powder
3/4 teaspoon salt

pinch of crumbled thyme
3/4 cup milk
1 egg
1/4 teaspoon Tabasco sauce
1 1/2 cups ground conch
vegetable oil
salt to taste

Melt the butter in a small skillet over low heat. Add the onion, green pepper and celery. Cook for 5 minutes or until the onion is tender, stirring occasionally. Combine the flour, baking powder, 3/4 teaspoon salt and thyme in a large bowl and mix well. Beat the milk, egg and Tabasco sauce in a small bowl. Add to the flour mixture and mix well. Add the onion mixture and conch and mix well. Cool until firm.

    Heat at least 2 inches of oil in a large skillet. Working with small batches, drop the conch mixture by tablespoonfuls into the hot oil. Fry until golden brown on both sides, turning as needed. Drain on paper towels and sprinkle lightly with salt to taste. Serve with Horseradish Sauce if desired.

Yield: 36 fritters

Horseradish Sauce

3/4 cup catsup
1/2 cup mayonnaise
1 tablespoon minced shallots
1/2 teaspoon Tabasco sauce
1 tablespoon drained
    prepared horseradish
1 tablespoon fresh lemon
    juice

Combine the catsup, mayonnaise, shallots, Tabasco sauce, horseradish and lemon juice in a bowl and mix well.

Yield: 1 1/2 cups

Chatham Club Original Bloody Mary Mix

3/4 teaspoon salt
1/4 cup lime juice or lemon juice
4 to 6 teaspoons Worcestershire sauce
8 to 10 drops of Tabasco sauce
1 teaspoon (rounded) prepared horseradish
V-8 juice

Combine the salt, lime juice, Worcestershire sauce, Tabasco sauce and horseradish in a 1-quart container and mix well. Add enough V-8 juice to fill the container and mix well. Store in the refrigerator. To serve, pour 3 tablespoons vodka into a glass and add ice. Fill with Bloody Mary Mix and garnish with a celery stalk.

Yield: 1 quart

Crab Quiche

2 unbaked (9 1/2-inch) pie shells
4 ounces Swiss cheese, shredded
2 tablespoons tomato paste
2 cups half-and-half
6 eggs
6 tablespoons butter or margarine
5 large shallots, minced
1/2 cup water
1 pound fresh crab meat, cooked
salt and white pepper to taste
6 tablespoons dry vermouth
4 ounces Swiss cheese, shredded

Prick the bottoms of the pie shells in several places. Sprinkle the bottom of each pie shell with half the 4 ounces cheese. Bake at 350 degrees until the cheese is melted. Remove from the oven. This step seals the pie shells to prevent sogginess.

Combine the tomato paste and half-and-half in a mixer bowl or food processor container and blend well. Add the eggs 2 at a time, blending well after each addition. Pour into a large bowl and set aside.

Melt the butter in a large skillet. Add the shallots and water and bring to a boil. Boil until the water has evaporated and the shallots are tender. Stir in the crab meat. Season with salt and white pepper. Add the vermouth and return to a boil.

Stir a small amount of the hot crab meat mixture into the egg mixture; stir the egg mixture into the crab meat mixture. Spoon into the pie shells. Bake at 350 degrees for 30 to 45 minutes or until slightly firm. Sprinkle half the remaining 4 ounces cheese over each quiche. Bake for 30 minutes longer.

Yield: 8 servings

Low-Country Shrimp and Sausage Stew

2 pounds large shrimp
1 tablespoon butter
chopped celery
chopped onion
6 tablespoons white wine
1 tablespoon tomato paste
2 cups clam juice
1 bay leaf
peppercorns to taste
1 tablespoon butter
1 pound andouille sausage or
    kielbasa, sliced
1 small red onion, sliced

4 cloves of garlic, chopped
1 cup beer
2 summer squash, cut into halves
    lengthwise, sliced
8 ounces fresh okra, sliced
1 (8-ounce) tomato, chopped
2 tablespoons chopped fresh basil
dash of Tabasco sauce
1 teaspoon Worcestershire sauce
salt and pepper to taste
2 tablespoons butter, cut into
    pieces

To make shrimp stock, peel and devein the shrimp, reserving the shells. Sauté the shells in 1 tablespoon butter in a skillet until the shells begin to turn pink. Add a small amount of celery and onion. Add the wine. Cook until the vegetables are tender, stirring frequently and scraping up any browned bits. Add the tomato paste, clam juice, bay leaf and peppercorns and mix well. Simmer for 20 minutes. Strain the stock through a sieve. Measure out 2 cups, reserving the remainder for another use.

Sauté the shrimp in 1 tablespoon butter in a skillet for 2 minutes. Add the sausage and toss together. Add the onion and garlic. Sauté for 1 minute. Add the beer. Cook until heated through, scraping up any browned bits. Stir in the squash, okra, tomato and basil and mix well. Stir in 2 cups shrimp stock. Simmer, covered, for 3 minutes or until the vegetables are tender. Season with Tabasco sauce, Worcestershire sauce, salt and pepper. Swirl in 2 tablespoons butter. Serve over fried grits cake or rice pilaf.

Yield: 4 servings

from Frank Harris of the River House Seafood Restaurant

Red Pepper Rémoulade

1 red bell pepper
1 cup mayonnaise
1/3 cup chili sauce
1 tablespoon prepared
  horseradish
2 dashes of Tabasco sauce
1 teaspoon Dijon mustard
1 tablespoon lemon juice
1 tablespoon Worcestershire
  sauce
1 tablespoon minced green
  onions

Bake the red pepper in an oven or roast over a gas flame until blackened. Place the pepper in a plastic bag or paper bag until cool. Peel carefully and cut into chunks. Purée the pepper in a food processor. Add the mayonnaise, chili sauce, horseradish, Tabasco sauce, Dijon mustard, lemon juice, Worcestershire sauce and green onions gradually, processing until of the desired consistency.

Yield: 1 1/2 to 2 cups

45 South Sautéed Lump Crab Cakes

1 red bell pepper, chopped
1/4 Vidalia onion, chopped
1 egg
1 teaspoon Dijon mustard
Red Pepper Rémoulade
dash of cayenne pepper
dash of white pepper
dash of salt

2 pounds jumbo lump crab meat,
  flaked
olive oil
1 head radicchio, shredded
1 head Belgian endive, shredded
60 small shrimp, cooked, peeled,
  deveined
1 tablespoon simple vinaigrette

Sauté the red pepper and onion in a nonstick skillet sprayed with nonstick cooking spray until the onion is translucent. Let cool. Combine the onion mixture, egg, Dijon mustard, 1 teaspoon of the Red Pepper Rémoulade, cayenne pepper, white pepper and salt in a bowl and mix well. Stir in the crab meat. Shape into small patties.

Heat the olive oil in a skillet. Sauté a few patties at a time in the hot olive oil until golden brown. Drain on paper towels.

Combine the radicchio, Belgian endive, shrimp and vinaigrette in a salad bowl and toss well. Serve with the crab cakes and remaining Red Pepper Rémoulade. Garnish each serving with chopped tomato and chopped chives.

Yield: 4 to 6 servings

Cajun Red Beans and Rice with Sausage

1 pound dried red kidney beans
2 pounds smoked sausage or
    ham, cut into 1-inch pieces
8 cups water
1 cup finely chopped celery
1 cup finely chopped onion
1 cup finely chopped green bell
    pepper

3 bay leaves
1 teaspoon Tabasco sauce
1 teaspoon white pepper
1 teaspoon dried thyme
2 cloves of garlic, minced
1/2 teaspoon dried oregano
1/4 teaspoon cayenne pepper
1/4 teaspoon black pepper

Rinse and sort the beans. Combine the beans with enough water to come 2 inches above the beans and soak overnight; drain well.

Combine the beans, sausage and 8 cups water in a 5- or 6-quart saucepan or Dutch oven. Add the celery, onion, green pepper, bay leaves, Tabasco sauce, white pepper, thyme, garlic, oregano, cayenne pepper and black pepper and mix well. Bring to a slow boil over medium-high heat. Simmer, covered, over low heat for 3 to 4 hours or until the beans are tender and the sausage is cooked through, stirring occasionally. Remove and discard the bay leaves. Serve over hot cooked rice with corn bread.

Editor's Note: For a thicker version of this dish, remove 1 cup of the beans after about 1 hour's cooking time. Mash the beans and return to the saucepan. Continue cooking as directed above.

Yield: 6 to 8 servings

In southern Louisiana, Monday traditionally was cleaning and laundry day. The women would get up in the morning, put on a pot of red beans, and go about their chores. To this day, cafés in that region still serve red beans and rice as regular Monday fare.

Merlot Thyme Glaze

4 cups quail stock or
    chicken stock
1 cup merlot
$^1/_2$ tablespoon chopped
    shallots
$^1/_2$ tablespoon chopped thyme
1 tablespoon olive oil

Boil the quail stock in a large saucepan until reduced by $^1/_2$. Boil the merlot in a medium saucepan until reduced by $^1/_2$. Sauté the shallots and thyme in the olive oil in a skillet until the shallots are tender. Add to the wine and mix gently. Add the wine mixture to the quail stock and mix gently.

Yield: 2$^1/_2$ cups

Quail with Corn Bread Pecan Stuffing

1 quail, cleaned
red wine
1 tablespoon chopped onion
1 tablespoon chopped celery
$^1/_2$ tablespoon chopped garlic
virgin olive oil
$^1/_2$ tablespoon chopped thyme
1 tablespoon chopped pecans
1 tablespoon corn kernels
3 to 4 tablespoons crumbled corn
    bread
1 egg, beaten
clarified butter (see Editor's Note)
$^1/_2$ cup chicken broth
Merlot Thyme Glaze

Rinse the quail and pat dry. Combine the quail with red wine to cover in a dish or pan. Marinate, covered, in the refrigerator for 1 to 2 hours.

Sauté the onion, celery and garlic in olive oil in a skillet for 2 to 3 minutes or until heated through. Add the thyme, pecans, corn kernels and corn bread and mix well. Stir in the egg.

Spoon the stuffing into the quail cavity and truss with wooden picks. Place the quail in a baking pan and brush with clarified butter. Pour the chicken broth around the quail. Bake at 350 degrees for 20 minutes. Spoon some of the Merlot Thyme Glaze over the quail. Bake for 5 minutes. Let stand for 15 to 20 minutes. Spoon the remaining glaze over the quail to serve.

Editor's Note: For clarified butter, melt unsalted butter slowly to evaporate most of the water. Skim off any foam from the top. Then pour off the clear butter, leaving behind the milky residue. This clear (clarified) butter is especially good for frying because it has a higher smoke point.

Yield: 1 serving

from Cedric Vanterpool
Executive Chef, DeSoto Hilton Hotel

B. J.'s Tomato Pie

2 eggs
1 1/2 cups half-and-half
1/4 teaspoon salt
1/4 teaspoon white pepper
1/8 teaspoon nutmeg
1 1/2 cups chopped onions
2 tablespoons bacon drippings
1 1/2 cups chopped tomatoes
1/2 cup chopped mixed red and
     green bell peppers
1 teaspoon dried thyme

1 (6-inch) sprig of rosemary
4 (3-inch) sprigs of parsley
1/2 cup chopped fresh basil
salt and white pepper to taste
1 baked (9-inch) deep-dish pie
     shell
thinly sliced Swiss cheese
3/4 cup shredded mozzarella
     cheese
crumbled crisp-cooked bacon

Whisk the eggs in a bowl. Add the half-and-half, salt, white pepper and nutmeg and whisk until mixed.

Sauté the onions in the bacon drippings in a 12-inch skillet until translucent but not browned. Add the tomatoes, bell peppers, thyme, rosemary, parsley and basil and mix well. Season with salt and white pepper to taste. Simmer, covered, over low to medium heat for 15 to 20 minutes or until the mixture is heated through and the flavors have blended. Remove and discard the rosemary and parsley sprigs.

Line the pie shell with Swiss cheese, overlapping the slices so that all the holes in the cheese are covered. Mix the tomato mixture and mozzarella cheese in a bowl. Spoon into the pie shell. Bake at 450 degrees for 10 minutes. Reduce the oven temperature to 350 degrees. Bake for 15 minutes. Serve hot or at room temperature.

Yield: 6 to 8 servings

Wild Rice Casserole

1 (16-ounce) package wild
    rice
1 medium onion, chopped
6 tablespoons butter
1 cup chopped parsley
2 eggs, lightly beaten
1¹/₂ cups shredded Cheddar
    cheese or Swiss cheese
1 cup milk
salt and pepper to taste

Rinse the rice under cold
running water for 2 minutes.
Boil in water to cover in a
saucepan for 30 minutes; drain
well. Steam the rice for 10 to 15
minutes or until tender. Sauté
the onion in the butter in a
saucepan. Stir in the parsley.
Sauté for 3 minutes. Stir in the
eggs, 1 cup cheese, milk, salt,
pepper and sautéed mixture.
Spoon into a buttered 3-quart
baking dish. Top with ¹/₂ cup
cheese. Bake at 350 degrees for
35 minutes.

Yield: 10 servings

Shrimp and Grits

The owner of Crook's Corner Restaurant in Chapel Hill, North Carolina, says this is their most requested recipe. The Tarheels really love it!

4 cups water
freshly grated nutmeg to taste
salt and pepper to taste
1 cup stone-ground yellow grits
    (see Editor's Note)
3 tablespoons unsalted butter
2 cups shredded sharp Cheddar
    cheese
1 pound fresh shrimp, peeled,
    deveined

6 slices bacon, chopped
peanut oil
2 cups sliced mushrooms
4 teaspoons lemon juice
2 tablespoons chopped parsley
1 cup thinly sliced scallions
1 large clove of garlic, minced

Bring the water to a boil in a large saucepan. Add nutmeg, salt and pepper. Stir in the grits gradually. Simmer for 40 minutes or until all the water has been absorbed, stirring frequently. Remove from the heat and stir in the butter and cheese.

Rinse the shrimp and pat dry. Fry the chopped bacon in a large skillet until browned; drain well. Heat a thin layer of peanut oil in the skillet until very hot. Add the shrimp. Cook until the shrimp turn pink. Add the mushrooms and lemon juice. Sauté briefly. Sprinkle with the bacon, parsley and scallions. Add the garlic and mix well. Sauté for 4 minutes.

Spoon the grits into a serving bowl. Add the shrimp mixture and mix well. Serve immediately.

Editor's Note: For richer, smoother grits, boil in a combination of chicken broth, water and whipping cream. Add a dash of cayenne pepper or Tabasco sauce to the grits if desired.

Yield: 4 servings

Louisville Bluegrass Pie

¹/₄ cup butter, softened
¹/₄ cup packed brown sugar
¹/₂ cup sugar
2 tablespoons flour
3 eggs
¹/₂ cup corn syrup
pinch of salt

1 teaspoon vanilla extract
¹/₄ cup bourbon
1 cup chopped English walnuts
1 cup chocolate chips
1 unbaked (9-inch) deep-dish pie
    shell

Cream the butter, brown sugar and sugar in a mixer bowl until light and fluffy. Add the flour and mix well. Beat in the eggs 1 at a time. Stir in the corn syrup, salt, vanilla and bourbon. Fold in the walnuts and chocolate chips. Spoon into the pie shell. Bake at 375 degrees for 40 minutes. Remove from the oven and let stand for 30 minutes or longer. Serve with vanilla ice cream or whipped cream. Rewarm the pie slightly before serving if desired.

Yield: 8 servings

Apricot Rum Cake

4 eggs
³/₄ cup vegetable oil
³/₄ cup apricot nectar
1 (2-layer) package yellow cake
    mix

³/₄ cup sugar
1¹/₄ cups butter or margarine
¹/₂ cup light or dark rum

Mix the eggs, oil and apricot nectar in a mixer bowl. Add the cake mix; beat at medium speed for 4 to 5 minutes or until blended and smooth. Spoon into a greased and floured 10-inch tube pan or bundt pan. Bake at 350 degrees for 45 minutes or until the cake tests done. Heat the sugar and butter in a saucepan until the the sugar is dissolved, stirring frequently. Stir in the rum. Spoon over the warm cake in the pan. Let stand for 1 hour before serving.

Yield: 12 to 16 servings

French Fantasies

Some of the most elegant dinner parties have had French themes, and many of the finest French composers have been featured in the Masterworks Concert Series. From Bizet and Ravel to Berlioz and Debussy, the range of music is reflected in the types of parties.

Seated black-tie dinners feature many courses and a plentitude of fine wines. Bistro affairs highlight charcuterie cassoulets. Crusty breads and lavishly rich desserts enhance well-sauced dishes. Wine tastings, hosted by local connoisseurs, have heightened our awareness of cabernets and merlots, chardonnays and sauvignon blancs, not to mention burgundies and Champagnes.

Romance is as emblematic of France as fine food. So opulent table settings, silver epergnes, lavish floral arrangements, and antique linens provide the surroundings for some of the city's most sophisticated dinners. A starry night and moss-laden oaks provide the backdrop for continental cuisine.

Contents

Menu

A French Affaire

Smoked Salmon Mousse
with Citrus Vodka
(page 30)

Raspberry Vinaigrette Salad
(page 66)

Country Braised Veal Shanks
with Carrots
(page 67)

Philip's Garlic Potatoes
(page 68)

Honey-Glazed Shallots
(page 67)

Philip's Apple Tart
(page 69)

Raspberry Vinaigrette Salad

(Salade de Framboises Vinaigrette)

*mixed salad greens, torn into
    bite-size pieces*
1 small package spiced pecans
1 small package dried cherries

*1 small can mandarin orange
    slices, drained*
Raspberry Vinaigrette

Arrange the salad greens on chilled salad plates. Top with spiced pecans
and dried cherries. Decorate each salad with mandarin orange slices.
Spoon a small amount of Raspberry Vinaigrette over each salad and
serve immediately.

Yield: 8 servings

Raspberry Vinaigrette

1/2 cup raspberry vinegar
salt and pepper to taste

*1 cup mixed olive oil and
    vegetable oil*

Combine the vinegar, salt and pepper in a bowl. Add the olive oil mixture
and mix well. If you wish to enhance the raspberry color of the vinaigrette,
add a few fresh raspberries or a small amount of raspberry jam.

Yield: 1 1/2 cups

Country Braised Veal Shanks with Carrots

(Jarrets de Veau aux Carottes)

1 bouquet garni (1 sprig of fresh
    thyme, or ½ teaspoon dried
    thyme; 6 sprigs of parsley;
    1 bay leaf)
4 (12- to 16-ounce) veal shanks
salt to taste
¼ cup vegetable oil
3 onions, cut into halves, thinly
    sliced
1½ pounds carrots, sliced
    diagonally into ¾-inch
    pieces
1 cup dry white wine
1 cup chicken stock
4 small tomatoes, peeled, seeded,
    chopped
freshly ground pepper to taste

Place the bouquet garni in a cheesecloth bag or tie with kitchen string. Sprinkle the veal with salt. Heat the oil over medium heat in a heavy Dutch oven just large enough to hold the veal. Add the veal. Cook for 5 to 7 minutes or until lightly browned on all sides. Remove the veal and keep warm.

Cook the onions and carrots in the drippings in the Dutch oven for 8 to 10 minutes or until the vegetables are tinged with brown, stirring constantly. Remove the carrots and onions and keep warm. Skim any fat from the drippings in the Dutch oven. Stir the wine and chicken stock into the drippings gradually, scraping up any browned bits. Return the veal to the Dutch oven and add the tomatoes and bouquet garni. Cover and bring to a boil; reduce the heat to low. Simmer for 1½ to 2 hours or until the veal is very tender and cooked through. Remove and discard the bouquet garni.

Use the cooking liquid as a sauce, skimming away any fat and seasoning with pepper and additional salt if needed. Place the veal on a serving platter and surround with the carrots and onions. Spoon some of the sauce over the veal and vegetables. Serve the remaining sauce on the side.

Yield: 4 servings

Honey-Glazed Shallots

(Échalotes Glacées au Miel)

1 tablespoon unsalted butter
1 tablespoon honey
1 pound shallots, peeled,
    sliced
1 cup chicken stock
salt and freshly ground
    pepper to taste

Melt the butter in a saucepan large enough to hold the shallots in a single layer. Add the honey, stirring until melted. Add the shallots, chicken stock and salt. Cook over low heat for 20 to 30 minutes or until the shallots are tender and the liquid has reduced to the consistency of a glaze, stirring occasionally. Season with pepper and additional salt if needed. Serve hot.

Yield: 4 to 6 servings

Philip's Garlic Potatoes

(Purée de Pommes Provençale)

4 heads garlic
olive oil
¼ teaspoon celery seeds
salt to taste
10 to 15 whole peppercorns

10 to 12 potatoes, peeled, cut
   into quarters
½ to 1 cup butter, softened
½ to ¾ cup whipping cream
pepper to taste

Peel most of the papery skin from the garlic and cut off ½ inch from the tops. Place in a baking dish just large enough to hold the garlic upright. Cover completely with olive oil and sprinkle with the celery seeds, salt and peppercorns. Bake at 400 degrees for 15 minutes. Reduce the oven temperature to 325 degrees. Bake for 15 to 25 minutes or until the garlic is tender. Let cool. Squeeze out the cloves of garlic through the top. Purée the garlic cloves in a food processor. Reserve the garlic oil for another use.

Boil the potatoes in salted water to cover in a saucepan for 20 to 40 minutes or until tender; drain well. Mash by hand with the garlic, butter and whipping cream. Season with pepper and additional salt if needed.

Yield: 8 servings

Philip's Apple Tart

(Tarte aux Pommes Frangipane)

1 sheet puff pastry
1 (7-ounce) package almond
    paste, cut into small pieces
$^1/_2$ to 1 cup sugar
6 tablespoons butter, cut into
    small pieces

4 egg yolks
2 to 3 medium apples, peeled,
    sliced
$^1/_2$ cup butter, sliced
apricot preserves, heated

Roll the puff pastry $^1/_8$ inch thick. Invert a dinner plate over the pastry and trim into a circle. Discard the pastry scraps or reserve for another use. Prick the pastry several times with a fork and place on a nonstick baking sheet. Mix the almond paste, sugar, 6 tablespoons butter and egg yolks in a food processor. Spread over the pastry. Bake using the pastry package directions.

Layer the apples in a circular pattern in a pie plate, placing several slices of $^1/_2$ cup butter between each layer. Bake at 350 degrees for 20 to 30 minutes or until the apples are tender. Let cool. Invert the apples onto the baked pastry and glaze with apricot preserves.

Yield: 8 to 12 servings

Menu

Days of Wine and Roses

Smoked Atlantic salmon

45 South Sautéed
Lump Crab Cakes
(page 56)

Dilled Shrimp (page 70)

Scallops Provençale
(page 71)

Pâté and cheeses

Rack of Lamb with
Madeira Sauce (page 77)

Crudités

Chocolate mousse

Dilled Shrimp

1½ *pounds large shrimp*
1 *(12-ounce) can beer*
3 *sprigs of dillweed*
10 *sprigs of parsley*

1 *clove of garlic, crushed*
pinch of allspice
Fresh Dill Sauce

Remove the heads from the shrimp, leaving the shells intact. Combine the beer, dillweed, parsley, garlic and allspice in a saucepan. Bring to a boil and add the shrimp. Cook for 1 to 2 minutes or just until the shrimp turn pink; do not overcook. Rinse the shrimp under cold water. Peel and devein the shrimp. Toss the shrimp with Fresh Dill Sauce in a bowl. Serve warm or at room temperature.

Yield: 8 to 12 appetizer servings, 4 main course servings

Fresh Dill Sauce

2 *tablespoons chopped dillweed*
2 *to 3 tablespoons freshly*
squeezed lemon juice

¼ *cup light virgin olive oil*
coarsely ground pepper to taste

Combine the dillweed, lemon juice, olive oil and pepper in a medium bowl and mix well.

Yield: ½ cup

Scallops Provençale

2 pounds whole bay scallops or
    sea scallops, cut into
    $^1/_4$-inch slices
salt and white pepper to taste
flour

2 tablespoons butter
3 tablespoons vegetable oil
$^1/_2$ cup clarified butter (see
    Editor's Note)
1 teaspoon finely chopped garlic

Rinse the scallops in cold water and pat dry. Season with salt and white pepper and coat with flour, shaking to remove any excess. Melt 2 tablespoons butter in a skillet over medium heat. Add the oil. Add the scallops in batches after the foam subsides. Sauté each batch until tender. Remove with a slotted spoon to a heated platter.

Heat the clarified butter in a 6- or 8-inch skillet until sizzling but not brown. Remove from the heat. Stir in the garlic. Spoon the garlic butter over the scallops. Garnish with chopped parsley and lemon wedges and serve immediately.

Editor's Note: For clarified butter, melt unsalted butter slowly to evaporate most of the water. Skim off any foam from the top. Then pour off the clear butter, leaving behind the milky residue. This clear (clarified) butter is especially good for frying because it has a higher smoke point.

Yield: 8 to 10 servings

Artichoke Mousseline

6 artichokes
2 to 4 quarts water
2 sprigs of rosemary
2 cloves of garlic

juice of 1 lemon
1 teaspoon salt
1 teaspoon black peppercorns
1 cup whipping cream

Combine the artichokes, water, rosemary, garlic, lemon juice, salt and peppercorns in a large saucepan. Cook for 45 minutes or until the artichokes are tender; drain well. Remove and discard the artichoke leaves. Scrape each artichoke to remove the choke, leaving only the bottoms. Chop the artichoke bottoms into pieces. Combine with the whipping cream in a saucepan. Cook over medium heat for 5 minutes, stirring occasionally. Purée in a blender. Adjust the seasonings. Serve with roasted meats.

Yield: 2 to 3 cups

from Chef Walter Dasher of the Chatham Club

Susan Mason's Kahlúa Baked Brie

1/2 cup melted butter
1 cup packed light brown sugar
1/2 cup Kahlúa

1 whole (14-inch) Brie
splash of Kahlúa
2 cups toasted pecan halves

Mix the melted butter, brown sugar and 1/2 cup Kahlúa in a bowl. Remove the top of the Brie and fill with the brown sugar mixture. Replace the top and place on a baking sheet. Bake at 350 degrees for 15 minutes. Remove from the oven. Top with a splash of Kahlúa and toasted pecans. Bake for 3 minutes. Serve with savory crackers or gingersnaps.

Yield: 30 to 50 servings

Oysters Jean Louise

36 freshly shucked oysters
1 pound spinach leaves
1/2 cup clarified butter (see
    Editor's Note, page 71)
1/4 cup minced shallots

1/2 cup chicken stock
3/4 cup whipping cream
salt and cracked pepper to taste
2 to 2 1/2 cups Béarnaise Sauce
3 Roma tomatoes, chopped

Place the oysters in a strainer over a bowl. Drain well, reserving the oyster liquor for another use. Chop the spinach, discarding the stems. Rinse the spinach in cool water and pat dry. Heat a sauté pan over medium heat. Add the butter and shallots. Sauté until the shallots are tender but not browned. Add the spinach and chicken stock. Sauté for 3 minutes or until the spinach is wilted. Remove from the heat and drain well. Add the whipping cream, salt and pepper and mix well.

Place 6 oysters in each of 6 individual baking dishes. Cover with the spinach mixture. Bake at 425 degrees for 8 minutes or until the edges of the oysters curl. Remove the oysters and spinach to serving plates. Spoon Béarnaise Sauce over the top. Place some chopped tomatoes in the center of each serving. Garnish with fresh thyme sprigs and chopped parsley. Serve with cocktail forks.

Yield: 6 servings

from Chef John Jawback, Jean Louise

Béarnaise Sauce

1/4 cup tarragon vinegar
2 tablespoons water
1 teaspoon dried tarragon
2 teaspoons grated onion
8 egg yolks
1/2 cup butter
1/2 cup clear soup stock
1 teaspoon salt
1/4 teaspoon paprika
2 sprigs of tarragon, minced

Heat the vinegar, water, dried tarragon and onion in a saucepan. Let cool. Pour into a double boiler. Add the egg yolks 1 at a time, mixing well after each addition. Cook until thickened and smooth, whisking constantly. Add the butter and soup stock gradually, stirring until the butter is melted. Season with the salt and paprika. Stir in the minced tarragon. For special occasions, you may wish to add 1 pound flaked crab meat to the sauce.

Yield: 2 to 2 1/2 cups

Cream Sauce

8 ounces mushrooms, cut
    into quarters
1 (10-ounce) package frozen
    artichoke hearts, cut into
    quarters
1 (7-ounce) can hearts of
    palm, drained, cut
    into thirds
1 (8-ounce) can sliced water
    chestnuts, drained
1 (10-ounce) can cream of
    asparagus soup
$^1/_2$ cup dry white wine
1 cup sour cream

Combine the mushrooms,
artichoke hearts, hearts of
palm, water chestnuts and soup
in a large saucepan and mix
well. Cook until bubbly and
heated through. Add the wine
and keep warm. Stir in the sour
cream just before serving time.

Yield: 8 servings

Chicken Breasts in Cream Sauce with Spring Vegetables

(Suprêmes de Volaille Crème Printanière)

4 boneless skinless chicken
    breasts, cut into halves
8 thin slices ham
8 thin slices Swiss cheese
2 medium tomatoes, seeded,
    chopped

$^1/_2$ teaspoon dried sage
$^1/_2$ cup fine dry bread crumbs
3 tablespoons grated Parmesan
    cheese
$^1/_4$ cup melted butter
Cream Sauce

Flatten the chicken into 5x5-inch pieces. Top each piece with a ham
slice, Swiss cheese slice, 1 to 2 teaspoons of the tomatoes and a sprinkle
of sage. Tuck in the sides and roll up as for jelly rolls. Mix the bread crumbs
and Parmesan cheese in a bowl. Dip each chicken piece into the melted
butter, then into the bread crumb mixture. Place in a buttered 9x13-inch
baking pan. Bake at 350 degrees for 40 to 45 minutes or until the chicken is
cooked through.

To serve, place each chicken roll on a serving plate and spoon Cream
Sauce over the top. Garnish with paprika and chopped parsley.

Yield: 8 servings

Chicken Liver Pâté

1 medium onion, finely chopped
1 clove of garlic, minced
1/2 cup melted butter
1 pound chicken livers
1 teaspoon salt

1/4 teaspoon freshly ground pepper
1/2 teaspoon mixed herbs
3 tablespoons brandy
1/2 cup butter, softened

Sauté the onion and garlic in the butter in a skillet. Add the chicken livers, salt, pepper and mixed herbs and mix well. Cook for 10 minutes or until the chicken livers are no longer pink on the inside. Process the chicken livers and brandy in a blender until smooth. Let cool. Cream 1/2 cup butter in a bowl. Mix into the liver mixture. Spoon into a serving dish. Serve with melba toast.

Yield: 6 servings

Duck Breasts with Cabernet Cassis Sauce

1 bottle full-bodied fruity cabernet
2 cups no-salt-added chicken
    stock
1 clove of garlic
3 whole cloves

3 tablespoons crème de cassis
1 tablespoon (or more) honey
vegetable oil
butter
8 boneless skinless duck breasts

Cook the wine, chicken stock, garlic, cloves and liqueur in a saucepan until reduced to 1 cup. Stir in the honey. Strain the sauce through a sieve. Keep warm. Place enough oil in a sauté pan to cover the bottom; add an equal amount of butter. Sauté the duck in the butter mixture for 2 to 3 minutes or just until pink, turning once. Remove from the heat and let stand for several minutes. Cut the duck crossgrain into 1/2-inch slices. Arrange the slices on a platter. Spoon sauce over the top. Serve the remaining sauce on the side.

Yield: 8 servings

Wild Rice Imperiale

1 (7-ounce) package wild
  rice mix
1 small jar pimento-stuffed
  green olives, drained,
  sliced
2 cups coarsely chopped
  pecans
1/2 cup butter

Cook the rice using the package
directions. Sauté the olives and
pecans in the butter in a skillet.
Add the rice and fluff with a
fork. Serve with wild game or
Cornish game hens.

Yield: 4 servings

Rabbit with Prunes

*This very French recipe was once prepared for a Christmas dinner in Argentina.
It was also prepared once with great difficulty in Bangladesh, where the
mushrooms were contributed by a Japanese person and the bacon by a
Canadian. The rabbits were raised by the seminarians at the Catholic Cathedral.*

1 pound mushrooms, sliced
1 tablespoon butter
1 tablespoon vegetable oil
8 ounces slab bacon
2 rabbits, cut up
salt and pepper to taste
2 tablespoons flour

2 large onions, chopped
1/4 cup flour
3 cups chicken stock
4 cups red wine
2 bay leaves
8 ounces pitted prunes

Sauté the mushrooms in the butter and oil in a heavy sauté pan until tender.
Remove the mushrooms and keep warm. Cut the bacon into strips 2 inches
long and 1/2-inch thick. Cook the bacon in the sauté pan until crisp. Remove
the bacon and set aside. Drain and reserve the bacon drippings.

Season the rabbit with salt and pepper and coat with 2 tablespoons
flour. Heat enough of the bacon drippings to cover the bottom of the sauté
pan. Add the rabbit in batches, adding additional bacon drippings if needed.
Cook until light golden brown. Remove and set aside. Cook the onion in
the drippings in the sauté pan until translucent, adding additional bacon
drippings if needed. Stir in 1/4 cup flour. Cook over low heat for 5 minutes,
stirring occasionally. Add the chicken stock and wine. Bring to a boil, stirring
constantly. If the sauce is too thick, thin with a mixture of chicken stock and
red wine. If the sauce is too thin, cook over high heat until reduced to the
desired consistency.

Combine the rabbit, bacon, bay leaves and mushrooms in a large
heavy Dutch oven. Add the wine mixture and mix well. Bake at 350 degrees
for 30 minutes. Add the prunes. Bake until the prunes are tender. Adjust
the seasonings.

Yield: 6 servings

Rack of Lamb with Madeira Sauce

6 cloves of garlic
1/2 cup olive oil
leaves of 1 large sprig of
    rosemary
2 racks of lamb, trimmed
2 tablespoons butter
1/4 cup minced shallots

1 clove of garlic, minced
2 (16-ounce) cans white beans
1 cup (about) chicken stock
salt to taste
pepper to taste
1 bay leaf
Madeira Sauce

Combine the garlic, olive oil and rosemary leaves in a blender container. Process until the garlic and rosemary are very finely chopped. Spread the mixture over the racks of lamb. Place the lamb in a resealable heavy-duty plastic bag; seal. Marinate in the refrigerator for several hours to overnight.

Melt the butter in a saucepan. Add the shallots. Sauté for 2 minutes. Add the garlic. Sauté for 1 minute. Drain the liquid from the beans into the saucepan. Add the chicken stock and mix well. Cook, covered, for 20 minutes. Add the beans and mix well. Season with salt and pepper. Cook for 15 minutes, adding additional chicken stock if needed. The beans can be prepared ahead and reheated at serving time.

Remove the lamb from the marinade, discarding the remaining marinade. Grill the lamb over hot coals for 25 to 30 minutes or to the desired degree of doneness. The lamb may instead be baked at 425 degrees for 25 to 30 minutes.

Slice the lamb into chops. Spoon the beans into the center of several chops. Drizzle Madeira Sauce over the chops.

Yield: 4 to 5 servings

Madeira Sauce

2 tablespoons butter
1/4 cup minced shallots
2 cups lamb stock or mixed
    chicken stock and beef
    stock
3/4 cup madeira
1 tablespoon arrowroot

Melt the butter in a medium saucepan. Add the shallots. Sauté for 3 to 5 minutes or until tender. Add the lamb stock and madeira and mix well. Cook for 20 minutes. The sauce may be prepared ahead up to this point. At serving time, bring the sauce to a boil, stirring constantly. Mix the arrowroot with a small amount of cold water and stir into the sauce. Return to a boil, stirring constantly.

Yield: 3 cups

Lafayette Peach Pecan Tart

1 recipe (1-crust) pie pastry	6 peaches
3 tablespoons butter	lemon juice
5 tablespoons flour	¹/₄ cup pecan halves
¹/₂ cup packed brown sugar	2 tablespoons brown sugar
1 egg	2 tablespoons butter
3 tablespoons hazelnut liqueur	1 cup peach preserves
1 cup pecan pieces	1 tablespoon peach liqueur

Line a 9-inch tart pan with the pastry, being careful not to roll the pastry down over the edge of the tart pan. Chill until needed.

Combine 3 tablespoons butter, flour, ¹/₂ cup brown sugar, egg and hazelnut liqueur in a food processor container. Process until smooth. Add 1 cup pecans. Process in short bursts until the pecans are finely chopped but not pulverized. Spoon into the pastry-lined tart pan. Return to the refrigerator until needed.

Peel and slice the peaches. Sprinkle lemon juice over the peach slices to prevent browning. Arrange the peach slices and ¹/₄ cup pecans in an attractive pattern in the tart pan, beginning at the center with the pecans overlapping the peach slices. Sprinkle with brown sugar and dot with butter. Bake at 400 degrees for 45 minutes or until light golden brown.

Melt the preserves in a small saucepan over low heat, stirring constantly with a wooden spoon. Strain through a fine sieve and return to the saucepan. Stir in the peach liqueur. Brush over the top of the tart to glaze. Serve at room temperature.

Yield: 8 servings

This recipe was developed to incorporate two typical Georgia ingredients in the French-style tart. The original would have been prepared with apples and almonds.

Pear Soufflé with Orange Custard Sauce

2 tablespoons sugar
2 (29-ounce) cans pear halves,
    drained
grated zest of 1 orange
1/3 cup sugar
1/2 cup water
2 teaspoons cornstarch
1 tablespoon lemon juice

8 egg whites, at room
    temperature
pinch of salt
1/4 teaspoon cream of tartar
1 tablespoon sugar
1/4 cup pear brandy
1 tablespoon confectioners' sugar

Butter the inside and edge of a 2-quart soufflé dish. Place 2 tablespoons sugar in the soufflé dish, tilting to coat the dish. Discard any excess sugar. Cut 2 of the pear halves into 1/4-inch cubes; set aside. Process the remaining pear halves and orange zest in a food processor fitted with a metal blade for 10 seconds or until puréed. Cook the purée in a saucepan over medium heat for 30 minutes or until thickened and reduced to 1 1/2 cups. Bring 1/3 cup sugar and water to a boil in a medium saucepan. Boil for 5 minutes or until syrupy. Dissolve the cornstarch in the lemon juice. Add the cornstarch and sugar syrup to the pear mixture. Cook until of the consistency of marmalade, stirring constantly. Remove to a large bowl.

Beat the egg whites in a mixer bowl until foamy. Add the salt and cream of tartar, beating constantly until stiff but not dry. Fold in 1 tablespoon sugar. Whisk 1/4 of the egg whites into the pear mixture. Fold the remaining egg whites into the pear mixture. Fold in the pear brandy. Spoon half the pear mixture into the soufflé dish. Sprinkle with 2/3 of the chopped pears. Add the remaining pear mixture, smoothing the top; the mixture should come to the top of the dish. Run a wooden spoon handle around the inside of the soufflé dish to make a groove. Sprinkle the remaining chopped pears over the top. Bake at 425 degrees for 16 minutes or until browned. Sift the confectioners' sugar over the top immediately. Remove from the oven and serve with chilled Orange Custard Sauce.

Yield: 8 servings

Orange Custard Sauce

2 cups milk
7 egg yolks
1/2 cup sugar
pinch of salt
zest of 2 oranges

Scald the milk in a nonreactive saucepan. Process the egg yolks, sugar and salt in a food processor fitted with a metal blade for 1 minute or until the mixture is thick and pale yellow. Add 1 cup of the scalded milk with the food processor running. Whisk a small amount of the remaining milk into the egg yolk mixture; whisk the egg yolk mixture into the remaining milk in the saucepan gradually. Add the orange zest. Cook over medium heat until thickened, stirring constantly; do not boil. Strain into a metal bowl and set the bowl over ice or in cold water to cool the custard quickly. Stir occasionally. Cover and chill thoroughly.

Yield: 2 cups

South of the Border

Many PARTIES A LA CARTE have had a Mexican theme and not only because of the great food and drinks. There is a gaiety, a true enjoyment, in the more relaxed atmosphere, a release of care and a real "mañana" atmosphere (sort of like Scarlett O'Hara's "I'll think about that tomorrow" attitude), which is ever present in the Latin culture.

Surely frosty Margaritas, ice-cold Mexican beer, and the creamy smoothness of custardy flan are delicious in and of themselves, but they are certainly necessary to offset the fiery chilis and tongue-tingling tastes of the hot foods served in south-of-the-border meals.

The music of such composers as Chavez and Villa-Lobos and the plaintive sounds of the classical guitar enhance the moods that accompany these meals. Castanets and flamenco dancing enliven the air.

The humid—nearly tropical—atmosphere that is present along the low-country coast is reflected in those lands to the south.

Contents

Menu

Juarez

Margaritas
(page 84)

Chili con Queso
(page 84)

Chicken Enchiladas
(page 85)

Chili con Carne
(page 88)

Mexican salsa

Frozen Strawberry Surprise
(page 90)

Margarita

1 1/2 ounces tequila
1/2 ounce Triple Sec
juice and peel of 1/2 lemon
    or lime
crushed ice
salt to taste

Process the tequila, Triple Sec,
lemon juice and crushed ice
in a blender. Rub the rim of a
3-ounce cocktail glass with the
lemon peel; dip the rim into
salt. Pour the tequila mixture
into the prepared glass.

Yield: 1 serving

Chile con Queso

2 pounds Velveeta cheese, cut
    into chunks
2 large onions, minced
1 (16-ounce) can tomatoes,
    drained, chopped

2 small cloves of garlic, minced
2 (4-ounce) cans chopped green
    chiles, drained
2 tablespoons Worcestershire
    sauce

Melt the cheese in a double boiler over hot water, stirring occasionally. Add
the onions, tomatoes, garlic, green chiles and Worcestershire sauce and mix
well. Cook for 30 minutes, stirring occasionally.

Serve as a dip with corn chips, or use as a topping for baked potatoes,
broccoli or other vegetables.

Yield: 6 cups

Chicken Enchiladas

1 (4-pound) chicken
2 cups sour cream
2 (10-ounce) cans cream of
  chicken soup
2 (4-ounce) cans chopped green
  chiles

2 bunches green onions, chopped
18 to 24 flour tortillas
8 ounces Monterey Jack cheese,
  shredded
16 ounces sharp Cheddar cheese,
  shredded

Combine the chicken with water to cover in a stockpot. Simmer until the chicken is tender; drain well. Remove and discard the chicken skin and bones. Chop the chicken into bite-size pieces.

Combine the chicken, sour cream, soup, undrained green chiles and green onions in a bowl and mix well. Place 2 tablespoonfuls of the chicken mixture on each tortilla. Top each with 1 tablespoon Monterey Jack cheese and 1 tablespoon Cheddar cheese. Roll up and place seam side down in a 9x13-inch glass baking dish. Spoon any remaining chicken mixture over the enchiladas. Sprinkle with any remaining cheese.

Bake, covered with foil, at 325 degrees for 30 minutes. Bake, uncovered, for 10 minutes or until the chicken is cooked through. Let stand for 5 to 10 minutes before serving.

Yield: 9 to 12 servings

Quick Chicken Enchiladas

2 large chicken breasts
1 cup chopped onion
1 clove of garlic, minced
2 tablespoons butter or
    margarine
1 (16-ounce) can tomatoes,
    chopped
1 (8-ounce) can tomato sauce
1/4 cup chopped green chiles

1 teaspoon sugar
1 teaspoon ground cumin
1/2 teaspoon dried oregano
1/2 teaspoon dried basil
12 flour tortillas
2 1/2 cups shredded Monterey Jack
    cheese
3/4 cup sour cream

Combine the chicken with water to cover in a saucepan. Simmer for 15 to 20 minutes or until tender; drain well. Remove and discard the chicken skin and bones. Cut the chicken into 12 strips.

Cook the onion and garlic in the butter in a saucepan until tender. Add the tomatoes, tomato sauce, green chiles, sugar, cumin, oregano and basil and mix well. Bring to a boil and reduce the heat. Simmer, covered, for 20 minutes. Remove from the heat.

Dip each tortilla into the tomato mixture to soften; shake to remove any excess. Place 1 strip of chicken and 2 tablespoons of the cheese on each tortilla. Roll up and place seam side down in a 9x13-inch baking dish. Stir the sour cream into the tomato mixture and spoon over the enchiladas. Sprinkle with the remaining cheese. Bake, covered, at 350 degrees for 40 minutes or until the chicken is cooked through.

Yield: 6 servings

Chiles Rellenos

4 whole canned green chiles
3 to 4 ounces Monterey Jack
    cheese or jalapeño Jack
    cheese
$1/4$ cup flour

salt and pepper to taste
3 egg yolks
3 egg whites, stiffly beaten
vegetable oil

Rinse the green chiles to remove any seeds. Cut the cheese into thin slices. Insert 1 slice of cheese into each green chile.

Mix the flour, salt and pepper in a shallow dish. Roll each green chile gently in the flour mixture and place on a waxed paper-lined pan. Chill for several hours.

Beat the egg yolks in a bowl until thick. Fold in the egg whites. Heat oil for deep-frying in a cast-iron skillet. Coat each stuffed chile with the egg mixture. Drop carefully into the hot oil. Fry until golden brown. Drain on paper towels. Serve immediately with salsa.

Yield: 4 servings

Chili con Carne

5 slices bacon
8 ounces Italian sausage, sliced
1½ pounds beef chuck, cut into
    cubes or coarsely ground
2 medium onions, chopped
1 green bell pepper, chopped
1 clove of garlic, minced
2 dried red chile peppers, seeded,
    crumbled

2 jalapeños, seeded, chopped
1 to 1½ tablespoons chili powder
¼ teaspoon dried oregano
salt to taste
2½ cups water
1 (12-ounce) can tomato paste
1 (16-ounce) can pinto beans,
    drained

Cook the bacon in a large saucepan or Dutch oven until crisp. Drain and crumble the bacon. Brown the sausage in the saucepan; drain, reserving 2 tablespoons of the drippings.

Add the beef cubes, onions, green pepper and garlic to the drippings in the saucepan and mix well. Cook until the beef is browned, stirring until crumbly; drain well. Add the crumbled bacon, sausage, chile peppers, jalapeños, chili powder, oregano and salt and mix well. Stir in the water and tomato paste. Bring to a boil. Simmer, covered, for 1½ hours, stirring occasionally. Stir in the beans. Simmer, covered, for 30 minutes.

Yield: 8 servings

Avocado Shrimp Boats

1 pound large shrimp, cooked,
   peeled
3 plum tomatoes, seeded, cut into
   $^1/_4$-inch pieces
juice of 1 lime
3 small avocados, cut into
   halves, pitted

1 cup pineapple cubes
1 cup canned mandarin orange
   sections
1 cup Cilantro Mayonnaise

Cut each shrimp into 3 to 4 pieces. Toss with the tomatoes in a large bowl.
Place the lime juice in a medium bowl. Remove 6 balls from each avocado
half with a small melon baller; toss with the lime juice. Rub the remaining
exposed avocados with lime juice to prevent discoloration. Add the avocado
balls, pineapple cubes, and orange sections to the shrimp mixture. Add the
Cilantro Mayonnaise and toss gently. Fill each avocado half with $^1/_2$ cup of
the shrimp mixture. Garnish with cilantro leaves.

Yield: 6 servings

Cilantro Mayonnaise

$^1/_2$ cup mayonnaise
2 tablespoons chopped fresh
   cilantro

$^1/_2$ cup sour cream
2 tablespoons chopped fresh
   parsley

Combine the mayonnaise, cilantro, sour cream and parsley in a bowl and
mix well.

Yield: 1$^1/_4$ cups

Frozen Strawberry Surprise

(Fresa Sorpresa)

1 cup flour
1/4 cup packed brown sugar
1/2 cup chopped walnuts
1/2 cup melted butter or
    margarine
2 egg whites

2 cups sliced strawberries (see
    Editor's Note)
1 cup sugar
2 tablespoons lemon juice
1 cup whipping cream, whipped

Combine the flour, brown sugar, walnuts and melted butter in a bowl and mix well. Spoon into a shallow baking pan. Bake at 350 degrees for 20 minutes, stirring occasionally. Let stand until cool enough to handle. Sprinkle 2/3 of the mixture into a 9x13-inch pan or 12 individual serving dishes.

Combine the egg whites, strawberries, sugar and lemon juice in a mixer bowl. Beat at high speed for 10 minutes. Fold in the whipped cream. Spoon over the crumbs in the pan. Top with the remaining crumbs. Freeze for 6 hours. Garnish with mint, strawberries or lemon peel.

Editor's Note: You may substitute one 10-ounce package of frozen strawberries for the fresh ones and reduce the sugar to 2/3 cup.

Yield: 12 servings

Cuban Black Bean Soup

1 pound black beans
12 cups water
salt to taste
4 ounces lean salt pork, cut into
    $^1/_4$-inch cubes
2 cups finely chopped onions
1 tablespoon finely chopped
    garlic
1 cup chopped green bell pepper

$^1/_2$ teaspoon oregano
1 teaspoon thyme
1 teaspoon sugar
1 teaspoon ground cumin
$^1/_2$ cup finely chopped cooked
    smoked ham
$^1/_2$ cup tomato paste
1 to 2 cups fresh or canned beef
    broth (optional)

Place the beans in a large bowl and add enough cold water to come 1 inch above the beans. Soak overnight; drain well. Combine the beans, 12 cups water and salt in a large kettle. Bring to a boil.

Heat the salt pork in a skillet until the fat melts. Add the onions, garlic and green pepper. Cook until the onions are wilted. Add the oregano, thyme, sugar, cumin, ham and tomato paste. Cook briefly.

Add the onion mixture to the beans and mix well. Cook for 1$^1/_2$ to 2 hours or until the beans are very tender, adding beef broth if needed. Serve very hot. Garnish with chopped hard-cooked egg white.

Yield: 10 servings

Spanish Bean Soup

8 ounces garbanzo beans
1 tablespoon salt
1 ham bone
2 quarts water
3 to 4 slices bacon
1 onion, chopped
1/2 teaspoon paprika

1 pound potatoes, peeled, cut into
    1/2-inch cubes
1/4 teaspoon saffron threads
salt to taste
1 large chorizo sausage, or
    2 small chorizo sausages

Combine the garbanzo beans with enough salted water to cover the beans and soak overnight; drain well. Combine the beans, ham bone and 2 quarts water in a stockpot. Simmer for 45 minutes, stirring occasionally.

Combine the bacon, onion and paprika in a skillet. Sauté until the onion is tender. Add the mixture to the beans. Add the potatoes, saffron and salt and mix well. Simmer until the potatoes are tender. Remove and discard the ham bone and turn off the heat. Slice the sausage thinly and stir into the soup.

Yield: 4 to 6 servings

This Cuban recipe comes from the Columbia Restaurant in Ybor City, Florida, a town noted for its cigar factories.

92

Spanish Fishermen's Rice Salad

1 pound mussels, cooked
1 (12-ounce) package saffron rice
    mix
3¹/₂ cups (about) chicken stock
3 pounds shrimp, cooked, peeled
8 ounces sea scallops, cooked,
    cut into halves
8 ounces tuna or other fresh fish,
    sautéed

1 cup chopped celery
1 cup chopped red onion or
    Vidalia onion
2 tablespoons chopped parsley
¹/₂ cup mayonnaise
¹/₂ cup sour cream
¹/₂ cup olive oil
2 tablespoons lemon juice
salt and pepper to taste

Remove the shells from the mussels. Line a deep bowl with upright mussel shells and set aside. Cook the saffron rice using the package directions, using the chicken stock as the liquid. Combine the mussels, rice mix, shrimp, scallops, tuna, celery, onion and parsley in a large bowl and mix well.

Combine the mayonnaise, sour cream, olive oil and lemon juice in a medium bowl and mix well. Season with salt and pepper. Stir the dressing into the salad and toss to mix. Spoon into the prepared deep bowl.

Yield: 8 to 12 servings

Corn, Tomato and Black Bean Salsa

1/2 cup finely chopped onion
1 teaspoon minced garlic
2 tablespoons olive oil
3 tablespoons chopped fresh
    cilantro
1/4 teaspoon ground cumin
1 jalapeño, minced
2 tablespoons cider vinegar
1 teaspoon salt
3/4 cup corn kernels
3 large Roma tomatoes,
    seeded, chopped
1 cup cooked black beans

Sauté the onion and garlic in
the olive oil in a skillet until
tender. Add the cilantro, cumin,
jalapeño, vinegar, salt, corn
kernels, tomatoes and beans
and mix well. Let stand for 30
to 45 minutes before serving to
allow the flavors to blend.

Yield: 5 servings

Seafood Enchiladas

1 (10-ounce) can cream of
    mushroom soup
1 (10-ounce) can cream of celery
    soup
2 cups sour cream
1 pound shrimp, cooked, cleaned
1 pound crab meat, flaked, or
    1 pound imitation crab meat
1 medium onion, chopped
1 (4-ounce) can chopped green
    chiles, drained
1 (4-ounce) can chopped black
    olives, drained
1 cup shredded Cheddar cheese
    or Monterey Jack cheese
1 to 1 1/2 cups coarsely chopped
    walnuts
garlic salt and pepper to taste
12 flour tortillas
1 to 2 cups shredded Cheddar
    cheese or Monterey Jack
    cheese

Combine the mushroom soup, celery soup and sour cream in a medium
bowl and mix well. Combine the shrimp, crab meat, onion, green chiles,
olives, 1 cup cheese, walnuts, garlic salt and pepper in a large bowl and
mix well.

Spread enough of the soup mixture into a 9x13-inch glass baking dish to
cover the bottom of the dish. Spoon the seafood mixture onto the tortillas.
Roll up and arrange in the baking dish. Spread the remaining soup mixture
evenly over the enchiladas. Sprinkle with 1 to 2 cups cheese. Bake at 350
degrees for 35 to 45 minutes or until heated through.

Yield: 6 to 8 servings

Cheese and Chile Rice

1 cup long grain white rice
1 (4-ounce) can chopped green
  chiles, drained
1 1/2 tablespoons chopped green
  onions

1/2 teaspoon salt
1 1/2 cups sour cream
2 medium tomatoes, thinly sliced
1 1/2 cups shredded Monterey Jack
  cheese

Cook the rice using the package directions. Stir the green chiles, green
onions and salt into the sour cream in a bowl. Alternate layers of the rice,
sour cream mixture, tomatoes and cheese in a buttered 2-quart baking dish
until all ingredients are used. Bake at 350 degrees for 30 minutes.

Yield: 6 servings

Guacamole

2 avocados, mashed
1 tablespoon lemon juice
1 tablespoon grated onion

1/2 teaspoon chili powder
mayonnaise

Combine the avocados, lemon juice, onion and chili powder in a bowl and
mix well. Stir in enough mayonnaise to make of the desired consistency. For
an especially attractive presentation, serve in a lettuce cup and garnish with
a sprig of cilantro.

Yield: 4 servings

Suzanna's Flan

1/2 to 3/4 cup sugar
3 eggs
3/4 cup sugar

1 tablespoon vanilla extract
2 (12-ounce) cans evaporated
milk

Heat 1/2 to 3/4 cup sugar in a flameproof casserole over low heat until the sugar has liquefied and started to brown, stirring constantly. Remove from the heat.

Beat the eggs in a bowl. Add 3/4 cup sugar and mix well. Add the vanilla and evaporated milk and mix well. Spoon the mixture over the caramelized sugar in the casserole. Place the casserole in a larger baking pan. Add enough boiling water to the pan to come 1 inch up the sides of the casserole.

Bake at 325 degrees for 45 minutes. Turn off the oven. Let the flan cool in the closed oven for 30 minutes or longer. Remove the casserole from the baking pan and chill overnight. Loosen the side of the flan from the casserole with a thin knife blade. Unmold the flan onto a serving plate.

Yield: 6 to 8 servings

Chocolate Rum Mousse

1¹/₂ cups light cream   3 tablespoons dark rum
5 eggs
1¹/₂ cups semisweet chocolate
   chips

Place the cream in a saucepan. Heat over medium heat until just below the boiling point. Set aside. Cook the eggs in simmering water in a saucepan for 1 minute or until coddled. Remove the egg yolks and beat well.

Combine the coddled egg yolks, chocolate chips and rum in a blender container or food processor container. Process until blended and smooth. Add the cream and blend well.

Pour the cream mixture into a bowl or individual serving dishes. Chill, covered, for 4 to 6 hours. Garnish with whipped cream and grated orange peel, nutmeg or grated chocolate.

Yield: 4 to 5 servings

Exotic Adventures

When Yo Yo Ma caresses his cello on the stage of the Johnny Mercer
Theatre or Midori draws her bow across the strings of her violin, Savannah
audiences can bask in the presence of two brilliant performers with roots
in the Far East. When the audience sighs to the sounds of Puccini's
Madama Butterfly, thoughts turn to an exotic nineteenth-century Japan,
a world of tea ceremonies and dark-eyed geisha.

Asia has been the focus of some of the Guild's most adventurous
PARTIES A LA CARTE: an Imperial Mandarin Dinner to celebrate the
Chinese New Year, complete with Peking duck; a Maharajah's Banquet,
featuring mulligatawny soup and tandoori chicken; and a Caravan
to Samarkand, an exotic feast redolent with spices that Marco Polo
would envy. When cruising the Pacific Rim, begin the evening with
a Singapore sling and then savor the flavors of a Malaysian lamb curry.
If a touring company of Anna and the King of Siam should come
to town, Thai food may be the choice for a dinner party
preceding the performance.

Contents

Menu

Cruising the Pacific Rim

Grilled Indonesian Satay with Sweet Peanut Sauce
(page 102)

Arranged Salad of Sautéed Sea Scallops on Napa Cabbage
(page 103)

Malaysian Lamb Curry with Condiments
(page 104)

Aromatic Rice Pilau
(page 105)

Tangerine sorbet

Hawaiian Pineapple Cake with Ginger Crème Chantilly
(page 106)

Gingerroot tea

Grilled Indonesian Satay with Sweet Peanut Sauce

8 ounces beef tenderloin
8 ounces chicken breast
8 ounces sugar snap peas
2 medium Vidalia onions or other
    sweet onions, chopped
2 cloves of garlic, chopped
2 teaspoons ground coriander
2 teaspoons ground cumin
2 teaspoons salt

2 dashes of Asian hot chili sauce
    or Tabasco sauce
juice of 2 lemons
$^1/_2$ cup peanut oil
$^1/_4$ cup chunky peanut butter
$^1/_4$ cup packed brown sugar
$^1/_4$ cup soy sauce
dash of Asian hot chili sauce
    (optional)

Soak forty-eight 6-inch bamboo skewers in water for 1 hour. Cut the beef and chicken into $^1/_4$-inch-thick 1x2-inch pieces. Place the beef, chicken and peas in separate bowls.

For the marinade, combine the onions, garlic, coriander, cumin, salt, 2 dashes of chili sauce, lemon juice and peanut oil in a food processor container. Process until puréed. Reserve half the marinade. Add enough of the remaining marinade to each bowl to coat each food lightly. Marinate, covered, in the refrigerator for up to 30 minutes.

For the sauce, combine the reserved marinade, peanut butter, brown sugar, soy sauce and 1 dash of chili sauce in a bowl and mix well.

Remove the beef, chicken and peas from the marinade, discarding the remaining marinade. Thread the beef, chicken and peas onto the skewers. Grill on a charcoal grill or gas grill until the chicken is cooked through. Serve with the peanut sauce.

Yield: 8 to 10 servings

Arranged Salad of Sautéed Sea Scallops on Napa Cabbage

30 to 36 scallops, about 1½
   inches in diameter
salt and white pepper to taste
olive oil
1 head napa cabbage, shredded
1 bunch cilantro, trimmed
Spicy Sesame Orange Vinaigrette

6 navel oranges, peeled, cut into
   sections
2 tablespoons toasted sesame
   seeds
2 star fruit, cut into ⅛-inch
   slices

Rinse the scallops and pat dry. Season the scallops with salt and white pepper. Heat a large nonstick skillet over medium-high heat until very hot. Brush the skillet very lightly with olive oil. Add the scallops and sear quickly; remove from the heat. Mix the cabbage and cilantro in a large bowl. Add the Spicy Sesame Orange Vinaigrette and toss to mix.

For each salad, place 2 orange sections on a serving plate. Top with about ½ cup of the cabbage mixture. Arrange 3 scallops in the center of the cabbage. Arrange 3 orange sections between the scallops and sprinkle with sesame seeds. Center a starfruit slice upright in the center of the mound. Serve immediately.

Yield: 10 to 12 servings

Spicy Sesame Orange Vinaigrette

¼ cup rice vinegar
1 tablespoon tomato paste
2 tablespoons frozen orange
   juice concentrate, thawed
1 teaspoon toasted sesame oil
2 tablespoons grated fresh
   ginger
2 tablespoons soy sauce
2 tablespoons peanut butter
1 teaspoon sugar
½ teaspoon (or more) red
   chili and garlic sauce
½ cup canola oil

Place the vinegar, tomato paste, orange juice concentrate, sesame oil, ginger, soy sauce, peanut butter, sugar, chili sauce and canola oil 1 ingredient at a time in a jar with a tight-fitting lid. Close the jar and shake well after each addition. Adjust seasonings. This vinaigrette keeps well in the refrigerator.

Yield: 1 cup

Malaysian Lamb Curry with Condiments

2 tablespoons butter
2 tablespoons peanut oil
3 pounds leg of lamb, cut into
    3/4-inch cubes
1 medium onion, chopped
2 plum tomatoes, peeled, seeded,
    chopped
2 unpeeled Japanese eggplant,
    cut into cubes
2 tart apples, peeled, cored,
    chopped
2 cups acorn squash cubes

1 large clove of garlic, minced
1 (14-ounce) can unsweetened
    light coconut milk
1 tablespoon Panang curry paste
1 teaspoon salt
1 cup boiling water
1 block mild S & B Curry Sauce
    Mix, cut into cubes
Aromatic Rice Pilau (page 105)
1 cup lightly packed shredded
    basil

Heat the butter and peanut oil in a Dutch oven. Add the lamb cubes in batches. Cook until browned on all sides. Remove the lamb and keep warm. Add the onion, tomatoes, eggplant, apples, squash and garlic 1 ingredient at a time to the Dutch oven, sautéing briefly after each addition. Return the lamb to the Dutch oven. Whisk the coconut milk, curry paste and salt in a bowl and add to the lamb mixture. Bring to a boil and reduce the heat. Simmer, covered, for 45 minutes or until the lamb is tender and cooked through, stirring gently at intervals. Add the boiling water to the lamb mixture. Push the lamb to the side and add the cubed curry sauce mix. Cook until the sauce is thickened and the cubes have dissolved, stirring gently at frequent intervals. Mix gently to incorporate the lamb.

To serve, place portions of the lamb curry in the center of warmed plates or oversize soup plates. Top with a scoop of Aromatic Rice Pilau and sprinkle generously with basil. Serve with the following condiments: homemade chutney or Major Grey's Chutney; toasted flaked coconut; coarsely chopped salted dry-roasted peanuts; and Minted Onion Raita (see page 105).

Yield: 8 to 10 servings

Aromatic Rice Pilau

4 cups water
4 whole cloves
1 cinnamon stick
$^1/_8$ teaspoon powdered saffron
$^1/_8$ teaspoon turmeric
4 chicken bouillon cubes

$^1/_4$ cup butter
2 cups converted rice
1 tablespoon butter
$^1/_2$ cup slivered almonds
$^1/_4$ cup golden raisins
$^1/_4$ cup currants

Combine the water, cloves, cinnamon stick, saffron, turmeric and bouillon cubes in a saucepan and mix well. Bring to a boil and set aside to steep. Heat $^1/_4$ cup butter in a skillet. Add the rice. Sauté until translucent. Strain the steeped bouillon and add to the rice. Simmer, covered, for 18 minutes. Heat 1 tablespoon butter in a sauté pan. Add the almonds, raisins and currants. Sauté until the almonds are golden brown. Stir into the rice.

Yield: 8 to 10 servings

Minted Onion Raita

2 cups thinly sliced mild sweet
   onions
2 tablespoons lemon juice

$^1/_2$ teaspoon salt
$^1/_4$ cup plain yogurt
1 to 2 cups minced fresh mint

Combine the onion slices with boiling water to cover in a bowl. Let stand for 1 minute; drain well. Add the lemon juice, salt, yogurt and mint and toss to mix.

Yield: 2 to 3 cups

Pineapple Glaze

1 (6-ounce) can unsweetened
pineapple juice
3 tablespoons water
1/2 cup packed brown sugar
2 tablespoons butter
1 1/2 teaspoons fresh lemon
    juice

Combine the pineapple juice,
water, brown sugar and butter
in a small heavy saucepan and
mix well. Bring to a boil and
reduce the heat. Simmer for 7
to 10 minutes or until caramel
colored. Remove from the heat
and stir in the lemon juice.

Yield: 3/4 cup

Hawaiian Pineapple Cake with Ginger Crème Chantilly

1 1/2 cups sifted cake flour
1 1/2 teaspoons baking powder
1/2 teaspoon salt
1/2 cup buttermilk, at room
    temperature
1 teaspoon vanilla extract
1/2 cup butter, softened
1 1/3 cups sugar

3 eggs, at room temperature
1 egg yolk, at room temperature
1 (8-ounce) can juice-packed
    crushed pineapple, drained
2 teaspoons grated lemon peel
Pineapple Glaze
Ginger Crème Chantilly
    (page 107)

Grease and lightly flour a 9-inch round cake pan or spray with nonstick
baking spray. Line the bottom of the pan with parchment paper. Sift the
flour, baking powder and salt together twice and set aside. Mix the
buttermilk and vanilla in a small bowl and set aside.

Beat the butter in a mixer bowl at medium-high speed for 3 minutes or
until light. Add the sugar gradually, beating constantly until light and fluffy.
Add the eggs and egg yolk 1 at a time, beating for 30 seconds after each
addition. Add the flour mixture and buttermilk mixture 1/2 at a time to the
creamed mixture, beating well after each addition. Fold in the pineapple
and lemon peel. Spoon the batter into the prepared pan. Bake at 350 degrees
for 35 minutes or until a wooden pick inserted near the center comes out
clean. Cool in the pan for 5 minutes. Remove to a wire rack placed on a
baking sheet.

Brush warm Pineapple Glaze over the warm cake. To serve, place a
small pool of glaze on each serving plate. Top with a cake slice and spoon a
small amount of Ginger Crème Chantilly over the top.

Yield: 8 to 10 servings

Lemon Grass Chicken Satay

(Takri Gai)

The term "satay" refers to the Southeast Asian method of cooking or barbecuing food on skewers.

1 pound chicken
2 cloves of garlic, chopped
½ onion, chopped
1 tablespoon palm sugar or
    brown sugar
juice of 1 lime
1 tablespoon fish sauce
tender portion of 2 strands of
    lemon grass, finely chopped
1 tablespoon vegetable oil
½ cup chunky peanut butter

1 onion, finely chopped
1 cup unsweetened coconut milk
1 tablespoon palm sugar or
    brown sugar
1 teaspoon cayenne pepper
1 stalk lemon grass, finely
    chopped
1 tablespoon fish sauce
1 tablespoon dark sweet soy
    sauce

Soak 12-inch wooden skewers in water for 1 hour. Slice the chicken very thinly; cut the slices into strips ½ inch wide and 2 inches long.

For the marinade, combine the garlic, ½ onion, 1 tablespoon sugar, lime juice, fish sauce, 2 strands lemon grass and oil in a food processor container or blender container. Process until blended and smooth. Thread 3 to 4 chicken strips onto each skewer and place in a large shallow dish. Pour the marinade over the chicken. Marinate, covered, in the refrigerator for 30 to 60 minutes, rotating each skewer occasionally. For the sauce, combine the peanut butter, 1 onion, coconut milk, 1 tablespoon sugar, cayenne pepper, 1 stalk lemon grass, fish sauce and soy sauce in a saucepan. Bring to a boil, stirring constantly. Keep warm.

Remove the skewers from the marinade, discarding the remaining marinade. Place the skewers on a grill rack and grill until the chicken is cooked through. Pour the sauce into small bowls to serve with the satay.

Yield: 6 servings

Ginger Crème Chantilly

1 cup very cold whipping
    cream
2 tablespoons sugar
½ teaspoon vanilla extract
¼ cup chopped candied
    ginger

Beat the whipping cream in a medium mixer bowl until stiff peaks form. Fold in the sugar, vanilla and ginger.

Yield: 2¼ to 2½ cups

Menu

Thai One On!

Thai Marbled Summer Rolls

(Poh Pia)

2 tablespoons peanut oil
3 cloves of garlic, chopped
1/2 teaspoon minced ginger
1/2 cup ground pork
1 tablespoon fish sauce
1/2 teaspoon pepper
1/2 teaspoon salt
1/2 teaspoon cornstarch

1 1/2 cups minced cooked bay
   shrimp
2 scallions, finely chopped
1 1/2 teaspoons cornstarch
2 tablespoons water
1 (20-count) package spring roll
   wrappers
vegetable oil

For the filling, heat the peanut oil in a wok over medium heat. Add the garlic and ginger. Stir-fry until the garlic is golden brown. Add the pork. Stir-fry for 1 minute. Add the fish sauce, pepper, salt and 1/2 teaspoon cornstarch and mix well. Cook until the mixture begins to thicken, stirring constantly. Stir in the shrimp and scallions. Remove from the heat and let cool.

To assemble the rolls, dissolve 1 1/2 teaspoons cornstarch in the water. Separate the spring roll wrappers. Place 1 wrapper so that it resembles a baseball diamond with the point of home plate facing you. Brush the perimeter with a 1-inch ribbon of the diluted cornstarch. Place 1 spoonful of the filling between home plate and the pitcher's mound. Fold the backstop flap over the filling; fold the first and third base points to meet in the center. Roll up to the outfield flap. Fold the outfield flap over the roll, sealing with the cornstarch mixture if needed. Repeat with the remaining spring roll wrappers and filling.

Heat vegetable oil to 375 degrees in a wok, saucepan or skillet. Add the spring rolls in batches. Fry until crisp and golden brown. Drain well before serving. Serve with 2 sauces, preferably hoisin sauce and Thai peanut sauce.

Yield: 20 rolls

Shrimp Tossed with Fresh Ginger and Lemon Grass

(Yam Khing Sod)

1 to 1¹/₂ pounds jumbo shrimp,
    peeled, deveined, patted dry
freshly ground pepper to taste
hot pepper sauce to taste
¹/₂ cup virgin olive oil
3 tablespoons fresh ginger,
    peeled, julienned
4 large cloves of garlic, thinly
    sliced

white portion of fresh lemon
    grass, julienned
¹/₂ to 2 teaspoons crushed red
    pepper, or to taste
¹/₂ to ³/₄ cup peanuts, lightly
    crushed

Combine the shrimp, pepper and hot pepper sauce in a bowl and mix well.
Heat the olive oil in a wok or skillet. Add the shrimp. Stir-fry until the shrimp
turn slightly pink. Add the ginger and garlic. Stir-fry until the shrimp turn
pink and the garlic is golden brown. Remove to a colander and drain well.
Fold in the lemon grass and red pepper.

To serve, place the shrimp on a warm platter. Top with the peanuts
and garnish with lemon twists, parsley, radish roses or carrot curls. Serve
at room temperature.

Yield: 4 to 6 servings

Chicken Curry Won Tons

8 ounces ground chicken breast
   or ground turkey
1 teaspoon sherry or white wine
$^1/_4$ teaspoon pepper
$^1/_2$ teaspoon sesame seed oil
1 teaspoon cornstarch

1 egg yolk
1 scallion, finely chopped
$^3/_4$ teaspoon minced fresh ginger
40 won ton wrappers
3 to 4 cups peanut oil

Combine the ground chicken, sherry, pepper, sesame oil, cornstarch, egg yolk, scallion and ginger in a bowl and mix well. Place slightly less than 1 teaspoon in the center of each won ton wrapper. Fold the wrapper into halves to form a triangle. Bring the 2 longest points together; moisten 1 inner edge with a drop of water and pinch to seal. Set aside on waxed paper or parchment paper. Repeat with the remaining filling and won ton wrappers.

Heat the peanut oil to 375 degrees in a wok or skillet. Cook the won tons in batches in the hot oil until golden brown and crisp; drain on paper towels. Serve hot or at room temperature with plum sauce, sweet-and-sour sauce, or Chinese hot mustard with soy sauce. Won tons will not be crispy if they are served cold.

Yield: 40 won tons

Roast Red Pork

(Moo Daeng)

1 (2-pound) pork loin
$1/2$ teaspoon red food coloring
2 tablespoons water
1 tablespoon fish sauce
1 tablespoon soy sauce
2 tablespoons hoisin sauce
1 tablespoon sherry

1 tablespoon palm sugar or
   brown sugar
2 cloves of garlic, finely chopped
1 tablespoon minced fresh ginger
$1/2$ teaspoon five-spice powder
1 tablespoon sesame oil

Pat the pork dry and rub with a mixture of the food coloring and water. Combine the fish sauce, soy sauce, hoisin sauce, sherry, sugar, garlic, ginger, five-spice powder and sesame oil in a blender container or food processor container. Process at high speed for 30 seconds and pour into a shallow dish. Add the pork. Marinate, covered, in the refrigerator for 2 hours or longer, turning occasionally. Remove the pork from the marinade, reserving the remaining marinade.

Place the pork on a rack in a foil-lined medium baking dish. Bake at 450 degrees for 15 minutes. Reduce the oven temperature to 350 degrees. Bake for 1 hour or until a meat thermometer registers 185 degrees, basting frequently with the reserved marinade. Remove from the oven and let stand for 15 minutes. Slice thinly and layer on a platter. Garnish with coriander leaves. Serve with plain rice.

Yield: 6 servings

Ginger Garlic Stir-Fried Vegetables

(Ka Kratien Pak)

2 tablespoons canola oil
2 tablespoons minced ginger
4 cloves of garlic, minced
assorted fresh vegetables,
   cut into bite-size pieces
$1/2$ cup chicken broth
$1/4$ teaspoon lemon pepper
salt to taste

Heat a wok or skillet until medium-hot. Add the canola oil, tilting to coat the surface. Add the ginger and garlic. Stir-fry gently just until aromatic. Add any larger vegetables. Stir-fry until about half-cooked. Add any smaller vegetables. Stir-fry briefly. Add the chicken broth. Stir-fry until all vegetables are tender. Stir in the lemon pepper and salt. Some colorful vegetables for this dish include green beans, yellow squash, plum tomatoes and onions.

Yield: variable

111

Thai Tea Cakes

(Kanom)

1 1/2 cups unsweetened
    coconut milk
6 eggs, beaten
3/4 cup palm sugar or packed
    brown sugar
1/2 teaspoon salt

Combine the coconut milk, eggs, sugar and salt in a double boiler and mix well. Cook over high heat for 10 minutes or until the mixture resembles soft scrambled eggs, stirring constantly. Spoon into a greased baking dish. Bake at 350 degrees for 30 minutes. Broil for several minutes or until the top is golden brown. Let cool before cutting into small squares. Serve with Coconut Ginger Ice Cream.

Yield: 6 to 8 servings

Coconut Ginger Ice Cream

2 cups milk
2 cups whipping cream
5 (quarter-size) slices fresh ginger
1 cup sugar
2 to 3 egg yolks, beaten

2 tablespoons chopped stem
    ginger in syrup
3 tablespoons ginger syrup
1 cup toasted flaked coconut

Combine the milk, whipping cream and sliced ginger in a saucepan. Cook over low heat just until bubbling. Add the sugar, stirring until dissolved. Stir a small amount of the hot cream mixture into the egg yolks; stir the egg yolks into the cream mixture. Cook over low heat for 8 minutes, stirring frequently. Spoon into a large glass bowl or stainless steel bowl. Place plastic wrap directly on the surface of the custard. Chill for 6 hours or longer.

Remove the sliced ginger from the custard. Combine the custard, chopped ginger and ginger syrup in batches in a blender container or food processor container. Process until mixed. Pour into an ice cream freezer container. Freeze using the manufacturer's directions. Top with toasted coconut.

Yield: 6 to 8 servings

Mulligatawny Soup

This soup has nothing to do with mulligan stew, and it isn't even Irish.
It is a dish from southern India, and the name comes from
two Tamil words: "molegoo" (pepper) and "tunnee" (water). Pepper
water comes in dozens of varieties.

6 tablespoons butter
1 large onion, sliced
1 clove of garlic, minced
1 teaspoon turmeric
1 teaspoon red pepper flakes
1 teaspoon cumin seeds
1/2 teaspoon ground coriander
1/2 teaspoon ground ginger

1 chicken, cut into 8 pieces
1 teaspoon ground poppy seeds
2 (14-ounce) cans beef broth
3 (14-ounce) cans chicken broth
salt to taste
1 large onion, sliced
3 lemons, cut into wedges

Melt the butter in a large saucepan. Add 1 onion, garlic, turmeric, red pepper flakes, cumin seeds, coriander and ginger and mix well. Cook for 5 minutes. Add the chicken and mix well. Cook for 5 minutes or until the chicken is golden brown. Add the poppy seeds, beef broth, chicken broth, and salt and mix well.

Sauté 1 onion in a nonstick skillet. Add to the soup and mix well. Simmer, tightly covered, for 40 minutes or until the chicken is cooked through. Ladle into soup bowls. Serve a lemon wedge with each bowl so that guests can add lemon juice just before eating.

Yield: 6 to 8 servings

Yogurt with Onion, Cucumber and Tomato

(Raita)

1 medium cucumber, peeled
1 tablespoon chopped onion
1 tablespoon salt
1 small tomato, chopped
1 tablespoon chopped fresh
   cilantro or parsley
1 cup plain yogurt
1 teaspoon ground cumin,
   toasted

Cut the cucumber into halves lengthwise and scoop out the seeds. Cut the cucumber into 1/8x1/2-inch pieces. Mix the cucumber, onion and salt in a small bowl. Let stand for 5 minutes. Press any excess moisture from the mixture and remove to another bowl. Add the tomato and cilantro and mix well. Add the yogurt and toasted cumin and mix well. Chill, tightly covered, for 1 hour or longer.

Yield: 4 servings

113

Sukiyaki

1 bundle of bean thread noodles
1 pound beef flank steak or rib
    eye steak, partially frozen
$^1/_3$ cup vegetable oil
2 onions, cut into bite-size pieces
$^1/_2$ cup (or more) sugar
$^1/_2$ cup (or more) soy sauce
1 bunch scallions, cut into bite-
    size pieces
1 to 2 carrots, cut into bite-size
    pieces

1 (5-ounce) can sliced bamboo
    shoots, drained
1 head napa cabbage or celery
    cabbage, cut into bite-size
    pieces
fresh mushrooms, cut into bite-
    size pieces
other vegetables, cut into bite-size
    pieces (optional)
$^1/_2$ cup wine or water

Soak the noodles in warm water until softened; drain well. Cut the noodles into 6- to 7-inch lengths. Cut the beef into paper-thin slices; cut the slices into bite-size pieces.

Heat the oil in a hot sukiyaki pot or a deep electric skillet. Add the onions, beef, sugar and soy sauce. Stir-fry briefly and push to one side. Add the scallions, carrots, bamboo shoots, cabbage, mushrooms and any other vegetables. Stir-fry briefly. Add the noodles to soak up the flavorful pan drippings. Add the wine at any time if the mixture becomes too dry. Serve with hot steamed rice.

Yield: 8 servings

"Sukiyaki," a Japanese family reunion dish, means "to cook as one likes." In Japanese homes the sukiyaki pot is brought to the table and the food is prepared there, with everyone gathered around participating in the cooking and eating. Chopsticks are recommended for authenticity and ambience.

Curry in a Baked Egg Custard

(South African Bobotie)

1 thick slice white bread
1/2 cup milk
1 large onion, chopped
2 tablespoons olive oil
2 tablespoons (rounded) Curry
    Spice Mix or curry powder
2 pounds cooked ground turkey,
    lamb, beef, chicken or
    flaked fish
1 tablespoon apricot jam

1/4 cup lemon juice
1/4 cup raisins
12 almonds, cut into quarters
10 dried apricots
1 teaspoon salt
1/2 teaspoon pepper
6 lemon leaves or bay leaves
1/2 cup milk
2 eggs

Soak the bread in 1/2 cup milk; drain well and tear the bread into pieces. Sauté the onion in the olive oil in a skillet. Add the Curry Spice Mix. Cook for 2 minutes. Combine the turkey, bread, onion, apricot jam, lemon juice, raisins, almonds, apricots, salt and pepper in a bowl and mix well. Spoon into a casserole. Press the lemon leaves into the top.

    Beat 1/2 cup milk and eggs in a bowl and pour over the bread mixture. Bake at 375 degrees for 45 minutes or until bubbly and golden brown. Serve with yellow raisin rice, mango chutney and flaked coconut.

Yield: 6 to 8 servings

Curry Spice Mix

1 1/2 teaspoons ground cumin
3/8 teaspoon ground cayenne
    pepper
3/4 teaspoon ground
    cinnamon
3/8 teaspoon ground cloves
1 1/2 teaspoons ground
    coriander
3/8 teaspoon ground turmeric
3/4 teaspoon ground
    cardamom
3/8 teaspoon ground nutmeg

Combine all the spices in a bowl and mix well. Store in an airtight container.

Yield: 8 teaspoons

Mediterranean Feasts

Through the Pillars of Hercules into the blue Mediterranean, we can savor
a multitude of tastes and delight in the music of the Maestro and the
Masterworks. The great Italian composers—Rossini, Vivaldi, Respighi—their
works are what we have hastened to hear our own symphony orchestra perform.

Opera, too, has delighted us in Savannah, and Italian music fosters the desire
for true Italian pastas, olive oil, satisfying breads, and rich sauces. The wines
of Italy have enhanced some of our most elegant PARTIES A LA CARTE.
From the vineyards of Tuscany to the tomato dishes near the Amalfi
coast, all the regions of Italy have their specialties.

Embedded in the Mediterranean like gemstones, the Greek Islands produce an
abundance of rich and delicious foods. Cheeses and olives enrich everything,
and the country's exciting music provokes exuberant and festive dancing.

Those sunny lands bordered by water are mirrored by our own regional
coast, and the similarity causes a familiarity and an appreciation
of both foods and music.

Contents

Menu

The Greeks Had a Word for It

Stuffed Grape Leaves (page 120)

Caviar Dip (page 122)

Feta Cheese in Phyllo Triangles (page 121)

Greek condiments

Roasted Spring Lamb (page 122)

Spinach in Phyllo (page 124)

Artichokes with Butter Beans and Lemon Dill Sauce (page 125)

Greek salad

Greek bread

Baklava (page 126)

Finger Bars (page 127)

Finikia (page 128)

Almond Custard in Phyllo (page 129)

Stuffed Grape Leaves

(Dolmades)

1 pound ground chuck
8 ounces ground lamb
2 medium onions, finely chopped
1 cup chicken broth or vegetable
    juice cocktail
1 bunch scallions, minced
1 cup minced parsley
1 tablespoon minced fresh mint

1 tablespoon minced fresh
    dillweed
²/₃ cup rice
chicken broth
1 (16-ounce) jar grape leaves
juice of 1 lemon
3 eggs
juice of 2 lemons

For the filling, combine the ground chuck, ground lamb, onions, 1 cup chicken broth, scallions, parsley, mint, dillweed and rice in a bowl and mix well. Chill, covered, overnight.

Drain and rinse the grape leaves, removing and discarding the stems. Place the larger tougher leaves in the bottom of a Dutch oven. Place 1 tablespoon of the filling in the center of the dull side (vein side down) of 1 of the grape leaves. Fold over once and fold in the sides; roll tightly into a sausage shape. Place the roll in the Dutch oven and sprinkle with a small amount of lemon juice. Repeat with the remaining smaller leaves, filling and lemon juice. Layer the rolls in a circular fashion in the Dutch oven. Place a heatproof plate on top of the rolls and add enough chicken broth to reach the plate. Bring to a boil. Simmer for 45 minutes, adding additional chicken broth if needed. Let stand for 1 hour before removing the plate.

Drain the Dutch oven, reserving the cooking liquid. Remove the grape leaf rolls to a shallow serving bowl. Beat the eggs in a mixer bowl until frothy. Add the juice of 2 lemons and blend well. Stir a small amount of the hot cooking liquid into the eggs; stir the eggs into the hot liquid. Cook over low heat until the mixture registers 160 degrees on a candy thermometer. Spoon the sauce gently over the grape leaf rolls. Serve with yogurt.

Yield: 4 to 6 servings

Feta Cheese in Phyllo Triangles

(Trigona Tiropitas)

1 pound feta cheese, crumbled
8 ounces small curd cottage
   cheese
1/2 cup grated Romano cheese
8 ounces cream cheese, softened
5 eggs

pepper to taste
1 (16-ounce) package phyllo
   dough, thawed (see Editor's
   Note)
1 cup melted butter

For the filling, mash all the cheeses with a fork. Beat the eggs in a mixer bowl until frothy. Add all the cheeses and pepper and beat well.

To assemble the pastries, spread melted butter on 1 sheet of phyllo dough. Top with another sheet of dough and paint with melted butter. Cut the dough crosswise into 2-inch strips. Place 1 teaspoon of the filling at the end of each strip and fold diagonally into triangles as you would fold a flag. Brush the top with melted butter. Repeat with the remaining phyllo dough and filling, brushing each sheet of phyllo dough with melted butter. Place on an ungreased baking sheet.

Bake at 350 degrees for 30 minutes or until golden brown. These pastries may be frozen for up to 3 months. Do not thaw before baking.

Editor's Note: Thaw phyllo dough, unopened, in the refrigerator overnight. It dries out very quickly, so do not open the package until the filling has been prepared. Unroll the phyllo and cover it with a damp towel. Keep the unused portions covered until needed.

Yield: 3 to 4 dozen

Caviar Dip

(Tarama Meze)

2 tablespoons unflavored
    gelatin
1/4 cup cold water
1 (8-ounce) jar tarama
5 to 6 slices dry white bread,
    soaked, squeezed dry
1 small onion, chopped
1 cup (about) olive oil

Soften the gelatin in the cold water in a heatproof bowl. Set the bowl in a pan of hot water over low heat, stirring until dissolved. Cool to room temperature. Combine the tarama, bread, and onion in a food processor container. Add olive oil gradually with the food processor running; process to desired consistency. Stir into the gelatin. Spoon into an oiled 4 1/2- to 5-quart mold. Chill, covered, for 8 hours. Unmold onto a platter. Garnish with lemon and cucumber slices and radishes. Serve with plain crackers. Tarama (fish roe) can be found at Middle Eastern delis or markets.

Yield: 8 to 12 servings

Roasted Spring Lamb

(Arni Psito)

1/2 leg of lamb
2 cloves of garlic, sliced
1/4 cup fresh lemon juice
1/4 cup balsamic vinegar
1/2 cup olive oil

2 cloves of garlic, minced
1 1/2 teaspoons salt
1/2 teaspoon pepper
1 tablespoon oregano leaves

Place the lamb on a rack in a shallow roasting pan. Cut several slits in the lamb 1/2 inch wide and 2 inches deep. Insert 1 garlic slice into each slit.

Combine the lemon juice, balsamic vinegar, olive oil, minced garlic, salt, pepper and oregano in a saucepan and mix well. Heat slightly. Brush some of the olive oil mixture over the lamb.

Bake at 325 degrees for 12 to 15 minutes per pound or until a meat thermometer registers 130 to 140 degrees for rare, basting occasionally with the remaining olive oil mixture.

Remove the lamb to a heated platter and let stand for 15 to 20 minutes. Carve into slices. Garnish with lemon slices and fresh mint.

Yield: 6 servings

Orzo with Dill Gratin

1 pound orzo
2 unpeeled cloves of garlic
salt to taste
1 cup whipping cream
1 cup chicken broth
³/4 cup grated Parmesan cheese
  or Romano cheese
1 teaspoon minced fresh dillweed,
  or 1 basil leaf, minced

pepper to taste
¹/4 cup grated Parmesan cheese
  or Romano cheese
¹/4 cup dry bread crumbs
chopped parsley to taste
3 tablespoons cold unsalted
  butter

Boil the orzo and garlic in salted water in a saucepan for 10 minutes or until the pasta is al dente. Drain in a colander and rinse well, reserving the garlic.

Peel the reserved garlic and mash with the whipping cream in a large bowl. Add the chicken broth, ³/4 cup cheese and dillweed and mix well. Season with pepper and additional salt. Spoon into a 2-quart baking dish.

Toss ¹/4 cup cheese with the bread crumbs in a small bowl. Add parsley and toss again. Spread over the orzo and dot with the butter. Bake at 350 degrees for 1¹/4 hours or until bubbly and golden brown.

Yield: 10 servings

Spinach in Phyllo

(Spanakopita)

4 (10-ounce) packages frozen
    chopped spinach, thawed
1 pound feta cheese, crumbled
8 ounces cottage cheese
1 cup grated Romano cheese or
    Parmesan cheese
8 eggs, beaten
2 bunches scallions, chopped
1 cup chopped parsley

1 tablespoon chopped fresh mint
3 tablespoons chopped fresh
    dillweed
salt and pepper to taste
1 tablespoon vegetable oil
1 (16-ounce) package phyllo
    dough, thawed (see Editor's
    Note, page 121)
2 cups melted butter

For the filling, squeeze the spinach dry in a kitchen towel. Combine the spinach, feta cheese, cottage cheese, Romano cheese, eggs, scallions, parsley, mint, dillweed, salt and pepper in a bowl and mix well. Chill, covered, overnight.

To assemble, layer 10 sheets of phyllo dough in a buttered 12x16-inch baking pan, brushing each sheet with melted butter. Spread the filling over the 10th sheet. Add the remaining 10 sheets of phyllo dough, brushing each sheet with melted butter. Fold the edges over to seal tightly. Cut only the top 10 sheets of dough in square or diamond shapes.

Bake at 350 degrees for 45 minutes or until golden brown. Let cool and use the previous cuts as a guide to cut through all the layers. This dish may be frozen but must be thawed before baking. Baking time will be 30 to 60 minutes.

Yield: 30 servings

Artichokes with Butter Beans and Lemon Dill Sauce

(Aginares ke Koukia mé Lemoni Anithos Salsa)

This dish is especially good served with baked lamb, rice pilaf, and a feta cheese salad with tomato, cucumber, and onion.

white portion of 1 leek, chopped
1 rib celery with leaves, chopped
3 tablespoons olive oil
$^1/_2$ cup minced parsley
$^1/_4$ cup minced fresh dillweed
2 tablespoons lemon juice
1 (14-ounce) can chicken broth

1 (10-ounce) package frozen
    baby butter beans
1 (16-ounce) can artichoke
    hearts, drained, cut into
    halves
salt and pepper to taste

Sauté the leek and celery in the olive oil in a medium saucepan until golden brown. Add the parsley, dillweed, lemon juice and chicken broth and mix well. Add the butter beans. Cook for 20 minutes or until the butter beans are almost tender.

Add the artichokes to the butter bean mixture and mix well. Season with salt and pepper. Cook, covered, over low heat for 15 minutes.

Yield: 8 to 10 servings

Baklava

1 pound ground pecans or
   almonds
½ cup sugar
2 teaspoons cinnamon
1 (16-ounce) package phyllo
   dough, thawed (see Editor's
   Note, page 121)

2 cups clarified butter
   (see Editor's Note)
whole cloves
5 cups sugar
3 cups water
1 cup honey
juice of 1 lemon

For the filling, combine the ground pecans, ½ cup sugar and cinnamon in a bowl and mix well.

To assemble, layer 10 sheets of phyllo dough in a buttered 9x12-inch baking pan, brushing each sheet with clarified butter. Sprinkle ¼ of the filling over the top. Cover with 3 more layers of dough, using 3 sheets for each layer, brushing each sheet with clarified butter and sprinkling each layer with ¼ of the filling. Cover with the remaining sheet of phyllo dough. Chill, covered, for 25 minutes. Cut the baklava into diamond shapes, cutting through all the layers. Brush the top with clarified butter and insert a clove in the center of each piece. Bake at 325 degrees for 1 to 1½ hours or until lightly browned.

For the syrup, bring 5 cups sugar and water to a boil in a saucepan. Simmer for 15 minutes. Add the honey and lemon juice. Simmer for 5 minutes. Return to a slow boil. Let stand until cool. Spoon the syrup over the hot baklava until no more syrup can be absorbed.

Editor's Note: For clarified butter, melt unsalted butter slowly to evaporate most of the water. Skim off any foam from the top. Then pour off the clear butter, leaving behind the milky residue. This clear (clarified) butter is especially good for frying because it has a higher smoke point.

Yield: 24 servings

Finger Bars

(Paximádia)

$^1/_2$ cup butter, softened
$^1/_2$ cup vegetable oil
$1^1/_2$ cups sugar
3 eggs

1 tablespoon (rounded) baking
  powder
$5^1/_2$ cups (about) sifted flour

Beat the butter, oil and sugar in a mixer bowl for 8 to 10 minutes or until blended and smooth. Beat in the eggs 1 at a time. Stir in the baking powder. Add the flour gradually, kneading until a soft dough forms.

Divide the dough into 5 portions. Shape each portion into a long, narrow, flat loaf, about $2^1/_2$ inches wide and 1 inch thick. Place the loaves 2 inches apart on greased cookie sheets. Cut each loaf diagonally into $^1/_2$-inch slices.

Bake at 375 degrees for 20 minutes or until lightly browned. Remove from the oven and slice again through the cut marks while warm. Bake at 350 degrees until lightly toasted on both sides. Let cool. Store in an airtight container.

Yield: 5 dozen

Finikia

4 cups finely ground pecans
1 teaspoon cinnamon
1 tablespoon sugar
6 to 7 cups (about) flour
1 tablespoon cinnamon
2 teaspoons baking powder
1 teaspoon baking soda
1 cup butter, softened
1 cup vegetable oil

1 cup sugar
1 cup orange juice
1 jigger of orange liqueur
1 cup chopped pecans
2 cups sugar
1 cup water
1 (8-ounce) jar honey
1 cinnamon stick
2 tablespoons lemon juice

For the crumb coating, mix 4 cups pecans, 1 teaspoon cinnamon and 1 tablespoon sugar in a shallow bowl or dish and set aside.

For the cookies, sift the flour, 1 tablespoon cinnamon, baking powder and baking soda together and set aside. Beat the butter, oil and 1 cup sugar in a mixer bowl for 5 minutes. Add the orange juice and orange liqueur gradually and blend well. Add the flour mixture and mix well. Knead until the mixture forms a ball and pulls away from the side of the bowl, adding additional flour if needed. Pinch off small pieces of dough. Flatten the dough and roll into oval shapes, stuffing some of the 1 cup pecans into each piece. Place on an ungreased cookie sheet. Bake at 350 degrees for 20 to 25 minutes or until golden brown. Let cool.

For the syrup, boil 2 cups sugar and water in a saucepan for 10 minutes. Add the honey, cinnamon stick and lemon juice and mix well. Boil for 5 minutes. Reduce the heat to a simmer; keep the syrup simmering while dipping all the cookies.

Immerse 4 or 5 cookies in the simmering syrup for a few minutes, turning several times. Remove to a colander with a slotted spoon to drain slightly. Roll the dipped cookies in the crumb coating and place on a flat surface to cool.

Yield: 5 dozen

Anna Nichols tells us she used to laugh at her young son-in-law, who called these wonderful cookies "Phoenicians" . . . until she looked it up and found that these cookies were taken to Greece by the ancient Phoenicians and that "Finikia" is "Phoenician" in Greek!

Almond Custard in Phyllo

(Galactoboureko)

2 cups milk
2 tablespoons butter, softened
$^1/_2$ cup cream of rice
6 tablespoons sugar
3 eggs
6 tablespoons sugar
2 tablespoons cream of wheat
$^1/_4$ cup lightly toasted chopped
    almonds

1 teaspoon vanilla extract
1 teaspoon grated orange peel or
    lemon peel
$^1/_2$ (16-ounce) package phyllo
    dough, thawed (see Editor's
    Note, page 121)
$^1/_4$ cup melted butter
confectioners' sugar

For the filling, combine the milk, 2 tablespoons butter, cream of rice and 6 tablespoons sugar in a saucepan and mix well. Cook until very thick and creamy, stirring frequently. Set the saucepan into ice water to cool the cooked mixture. Beat the eggs in a mixer bowl until frothy. Add 6 tablespoons sugar, cream of wheat and almonds and beat well. Stir gently into the cooked mixture in the saucepan. Cook over low heat until of custard consistency, stirring occasionally. Stir in the vanilla and orange peel. Chill, covered, for 2 hours or longer.

To assemble the pastries, cut 1 sheet of phyllo dough crosswise into thirds and spread generously with melted butter. Place 1 tablespoon of the filling in the center of each piece. Fold in the sides and then the end as for a blintz. Continue with the remaining phyllo dough and filling.

Place the pastries in a buttered baking dish. Bake at 375 degrees for 20 minutes or until golden brown. Sprinkle the hot pastries generously with confectioners' sugar. These pastries may be frozen after they have cooled.

Yield: 20 servings

Greek Wedding Cookies

(Kourambiedes)

2 cups unsalted butter, softened
1/2 cup confectioners' sugar
1 egg white (optional)
1 jigger of whiskey
1/2 teaspoon almond extract
    (optional)

1 teaspoon vanilla extract
6 tablespoons toasted finely
    chopped almonds (optional)
4 cups sifted flour
3 cups sifted confectioners' sugar

Cream the butter and 1/2 cup confectioners' sugar in a mixer bowl for 15 minutes or until light and fluffy. Add the egg white, whiskey, almond extract, vanilla extract and almonds and beat well. Add the flour gradually, stirring until a soft dough forms.

Pinch off pieces of dough and shape into various designs such as crescents or rounds. Place the cookies 1 inch apart on an ungreased cookie sheet. Bake at 350 degrees for 20 minutes or until very lightly browned. Cool slightly before removing from the cookie sheet to a flat surface sprinkled with confectioners' sugar. Sprinkle confectioners' sugar over the cookies and let cool.

Yield: 5 dozen

Farfalle with Three Cheeses, Pancetta, Tomatoes and Baby Peas

2 tablespoons olive oil
4 large cloves of garlic, minced
1/2 teaspoon red pepper flakes
1 jalapeño, minced
2 cups finely chopped onions
1 teaspoon (rounded) dried basil
1 teaspoon (rounded) dried
  oregano
2/3 cup minced Italian parsley
1 pound fresh shiitake, enoki or
  oyster mushrooms, sliced
12 to 16 ounces farfalle (bow tie)
  pasta

Béchamel Sauce
2 (28-ounce) cans Italian plum
  tomatoes, drained, coarsely
  chopped
1 (10-ounce) package frozen
  baby peas
4 ounces pancetta or prosciutto,
  chopped
1/2 cup grated Parmesan cheese
2 tablespoons unsalted butter

Heat the olive oil in a skillet over medium heat. Add the garlic, red pepper flakes, jalapeño, onions, basil, oregano and most of the parsley. Sauté until the onions are translucent. Add the mushrooms. Cook for 10 minutes or until the mushrooms are tender. Remove the mixture to a large bowl.

Boil the pasta in water to cover in a stockpot for 3 to 5 minutes or until al dente. Drain well and toss with the Béchamel Sauce. Add the mushroom mixture, tomatoes and frozen peas. Stir in the pancetta. Spoon into a buttered shallow 4-quart baking dish. Sprinkle with the cheese and dot with the butter. Bake at 350 degrees for 35 to 45 minutes or until bubbly and heated through. Garnish with the remaining parsley.

Yield: 16 to 18 servings

Béchamel Sauce

1/4 cup unsalted butter
3 tablespoons flour
2 cups milk
1 cup grated Parmesan
  cheese
4 ounces Fontinella cheese,
  shredded
4 ounces Gorgonzola cheese,
  crumbled
salt and pepper to taste

Melt the butter in a saucepan. Stir in the flour gradually. Cook until thickened, stirring constantly. Stir in the milk. Cook until thick, whisking constantly. Add the cheeses 1 at a time, mixing gently after each addition. Cook until melted, stirring constantly. Season with salt and pepper. Let cool. Chill, covered, until needed.

Yield: 4 cups

Menu

A Chef's Tour of Florence, Italy

Rolled Stuffed Sirloin

(Manzo Ripiéno)

2 (10-ounce) packages frozen spinach, thawed, drained
1 (2-pound) sirloin, butterflied
2 ounces pancetta, cut into small pieces, or 2 ounces prosciutto, thinly sliced
3 cloves of garlic, finely chopped
10 sprigs of Italian parsley, finely chopped
3 large eggs, hard-cooked
salt and freshly ground pepper to taste
1/4 cup freshly grated Parmesan cheese
1/4 cup unsalted butter
2 tablespoons olive oil
1/2 cup dry red wine

Cook the spinach using the package directions. Drain the spinach, squeezing out the moisture. Chop finely.

Place the sirloin between sheets of damp waxed paper and flatten with a meat mallet. Place the sirloin on a wooden board. Spread the spinach on the sirloin and top with the pancetta. Sprinkle with a mixture of the garlic and parsley. Cut the eggs lengthwise into quarters and arrange over the sirloin. Season with salt and pepper and top with the cheese. Roll up the sirloin and tie with kitchen string at 1- to 1 1/2-inch intervals.

Heat the butter and olive oil in a Dutch oven. Add the sirloin. Cook for 15 minutes or until golden brown, turning frequently. Add the wine and additional salt and pepper. Simmer, covered, for 15 to 20 minutes or to desired degree of doneness, turning 2 to 3 times.

Remove from the heat and cool for 2 hours. Cut into 2-inch slices to serve. This dish may be prepared up to 24 hours ahead, but bring to room temperature before serving.

Yield: 20 slices

Lamb with Black Olives

(Agnello con Olive Nere)

1 (3¹/₂-pound) leg of lamb, boned
salt and pepper to taste
2 tablespoons olive oil
1 onion, chopped
6 cloves of garlic, crushed
1 cup canned plum tomatoes,
   chopped

8 sprigs of thyme
1 cup (about) dry white wine
4 ounces pitted niçoise olives
2 anchovy fillets, chopped

Trim any loose fat from the lamb. Season the lamb with salt and pepper. Heat the olive oil in a Dutch oven and add the lamb. Cook over medium heat until browned on all sides. Remove the lamb and keep warm.

Add the onion to the drippings in the Dutch oven. Cook until tender. Add the garlic, tomatoes and thyme. Add just enough of the wine to moisten. Add the lamb. Simmer, covered, for 1¹/₂ hours, turning occasionally and moistening with wine. Add the olives and anchovies. Simmer, covered, for 30 minutes, basting frequently. Remove the lamb and slice. Serve the pan drippings as a sauce.

Yield: 6 to 8 servings

Bread Salad

(Panzanella)

1 (1-pound) loaf dry Italian
    bread (see Editor's Note)
1 red onion, sliced
10 fresh basil leaves
1/2 red bell pepper, chopped
1/2 green bell pepper, chopped
1 small zucchini, chopped
1 cup peas

2 tablespoons drained capers
2 large tomatoes, chopped
6 tablespoons olive oil
2 tablespoons red wine vinegar
1 clove of garlic, finely chopped
1/2 teaspoon salt, or to taste
freshly ground pepper to taste

Tear the bread into large chunks into a large bowl. Cover the bread with cold water. Place the onion slices and basil leaves on top. Let stand for 20 minutes.

Remove the onion slices and pat dry. Finely chop the onion slices into a medium bowl. Remove the basil leaves and pat dry. Tear each leaf into 2 to 3 pieces and set aside.

Squeeze the water from the bread and place the bread in a large bowl. Add the red pepper, green pepper, zucchini, peas and capers to the onion slices and toss gently. Spoon the mixture over the bread. Sprinkle the basil over the top, then the tomatoes. Chill, covered, for 2 hours or longer.

Combine the olive oil, vinegar, garlic, salt and pepper in a small bowl and mix well. Pour over the salad and toss to mix.

Editor's Note: The original recipe called for 2-day-old Tuscan-style bread, but any Italian bread should work nicely.

Yield: 8 to 12 servings

Grape Bread

(Schiacciata con L'Uva)

2 packages active dry yeast	pinch of salt
1 cup lukewarm (105 to 110 degrees) water	3 tablespoons olive oil
	$^2/_3$ cup chopped walnuts
3 cups (about) bread flour	2 tablespoons fresh rosemary
$^1/_4$ cup sugar	1 cup seedless dark red grapes

Sprinkle the yeast over the lukewarm water in a small bowl. Let stand for 10 minutes or until the yeast is dissolved and the mixture is foamy.

Place the flour in a large bowl and make a well in the center. Pour in the yeast mixture and add the sugar and salt. Stir with a fork, gradually working in all the flour. Knead the dough on a lightly floured surface for 5 minutes or until smooth and elastic. Shape into a ball and place in a medium bowl. Cover with a towel or plastic wrap. Let rise in a warm place for 2 hours or until doubled in bulk.

Heat the olive oil in a small skillet over low heat. Add the walnuts and rosemary and cook until the walnuts are toasted. Remove and let cool.

Turn the dough onto a floured surface. Punch down the dough. Knead in the walnut mixture. Pat the dough into an oiled 9-inch springform pan. Top with the grapes, pressing the grapes into the dough. Let rise for 30 minutes or until doubled in bulk. Bake at 400 degrees for 30 to 40 minutes or until browned.

Yield: 15 to 18 servings

Rice Ring Filled with Fruit

(Ciambella di Frutta)

1 orange
1 quart milk
1¹/₂ cups arborio rice
1 teaspoon vanilla extract
pinch of salt
1 tablespoon unsalted butter
6 medium plums, cut into
   quarters
3 large peaches or nectarines,
   peeled, cut into quarters

¹/₄ cup golden raisins
¹/₄ cup sugar
grated peel of 1 lemon
¹/₄ cup dry red wine
1¹/₂ teaspoons ground cinnamon
3 tablespoons sugar
2 eggs
2 egg yolks
¹/₄ cup sugar
¹/₄ cup light rum, heated

Peel and chop the orange. Grate the peel and set aside. Combine the milk and rice in a large heavy saucepan. Add the vanilla and salt and bring just to a boil over medium heat. Stir in the butter. Simmer for 10 to 12 minutes, stirring occasionally. Remove from the heat and let stand for 10 minutes. Drain in a colander and cool completely. Remove to a large bowl.

For the filling, mix the plums, peaches, raisins, ¹/₄ cup sugar, lemon peel and wine in a heavy saucepan. Simmer for 15 minutes. Add the orange. Simmer for 15 minutes. Remove from the heat; cool completely. Chill, covered, until needed. For the rice ring, mix the orange peel, cinnamon, 3 tablespoons sugar, eggs and egg yolks in a bowl. Add to the rice mixture and mix well. Coat a buttered tube pan with ¹/₄ cup sugar.

To assemble, arrange ³/₄ of the rice mixture around the bottom and side of the prepared tube pan. Drain the chilled filling and spoon into the cavity of the tube pan. Cover the filling with the remaining rice mixture and smooth the top. Sprinkle with additional sugar. Place the tube pan in a large roasting pan. Pour 4 to 5 cups lukewarm water into the roasting pan. Bake at 400 degrees for 45 to 50 minutes or until set. Remove the tube pan from the water bath and cool for 15 minutes. Unmold the rice ring onto a flameproof large serving dish. Spoon warm rum over the top. Flambé if desired.

Yield: 12 servings

Fresh Fruit Tart

(Crostata di Frutta)

1 1/3 cups all-purpose flour
2/3 cup cake flour
1 teaspoon (scant) salt
1/2 cup cold butter, cut into 1/2-
   inch cubes
2 egg yolks
4 tablespoons whipping cream
1/2 teaspoon almond extract
1 cup half-and-half
1 cup buttermilk
1 teaspoon vanilla extract
2 tablespoons sugar

4 egg yolks
1 tablespoon all-purpose flour
8 apricots, nectarines or peaches,
   peeled, cut into halves
1/2 cup sugar
2 cups raspberries
2 cups blackberries
2 cups blueberries
2 tablespoons Grand Marnier
2 tablespoons sugar
1 egg, beaten
1/4 teaspoon salt

For the dough, mix 1 1/3 cups all-purpose flour, cake flour and 1 teaspoon
salt in a food processor. Add the butter; process until crumbly. Add 2 egg
yolks, whipping cream and almond extract. Process in 10-second bursts
until a dough forms. Shape the dough into a ball; place in a bowl. Cover and
chill thoroughly. For the custard, whisk the half-and-half and buttermilk in
a bowl. Whisk in the vanilla, 2 tablespoons sugar, 4 egg yolks and 1 tablespoon all-purpose flour. Chill, covered, until needed. For the fruit, toss the
apricots with 1/2 cup sugar. Toss the raspberries with 1 tablespoon Grand
Marnier and 1 tablespoon sugar. Repeat for the blackberries and the
blueberries. Roll the dough into a circle on a floured surface. Fit into a
12- to 14-inch tart pan; prick lightly with a fork. Bake at 400 degrees for
12 minutes. Remove from the oven and brush with a mixture of 1 egg and
1/4 teaspoon salt. Bake for 5 minutes. Remove from the oven. Arrange the
apricots in overlapping concentric circles, beginning at the outer edge of
the tart shell and moving toward the center. Place the blueberries in the
center. Arrange the raspberries and blackberries around the blueberries.
Spoon the custard over the fruit. Bake for 45 to 55 minutes or until set. Let
cool before serving.

Yield: 15 to 18 servings

Scott's Olivada

3/4 cup pitted kalamata olives
1/4 cup pitted black
California olives
2 to 3 tablespoons sun-dried
tomatoes in oil
1 small clove of garlic
1/4 cup chopped yellow onion

Combine the olives, sun-dried
tomatoes, garlic and onion in a
food processor container and
process until mixed. Serve with
crackers or bruschetta.

Yield: 1 to 1 1/4 cups

Roasted Vegetable Minestrone

olive oil
1 medium eggplant, very thinly
sliced
1 medium zucchini, very thinly
sliced
1 medium yellow squash, very
thinly sliced
herbes de Provence to taste
salt to taste
1 large portobella mushroom,
trimmed
1 red bell pepper, cut into
quarters lengthwise
1 yellow bell pepper, cut into
quarters lengthwise

1 red onion, very thinly sliced
2 cloves of garlic, minced
1/2 cup red wine
2 cups beef stock
2 cups crushed tomatoes
1 (16-ounce) can kidney beans or
white cannellini beans,
drained
3 small bunches arugula or
broccoli rabe, coarsely
chopped
1 package fresh four-cheese
tortellini, cooked, drained
freshly grated Parmesan cheese

Brush a baking sheet lightly with olive oil. Place a single layer of eggplant,
zucchini and yellow squash on the baking sheet. Brush lightly with olive oil
and sprinkle lightly with herbes de Provence and salt. Bake at 400 degrees
until the vegetables are a deep golden brown. Place the mushroom on a
lightly oiled baking sheet. Rub the mushroom with olive oil and sprinkle
with herbes de Provence and salt. Bake at 400 degrees until tender and juicy.
Place the red pepper and yellow pepper on a lightly oiled baking sheet. Bake
at 400 degrees until blackened. Place the peppers in a plastic bag until cool
enough to peel. Toss the onion with olive oil, herbes de Provence and salt
in a small bowl. Place the onion on a lightly oiled baking sheet. Bake at
400 degrees until browned. Coarsely chop all the roasted vegetables.
Combine the roasted vegetables, garlic, wine, beef stock, tomatoes, kidney
beans, arugula and tortellini in a 6-quart stockpot. Cook until
heated through, stirring occasionally. Ladle into bowls and sprinkle with
Parmesan cheese.

Yield: 10 servings

from Bonnie Retsas, chef-owner of Soho South Cafe

Flounder Neapolitan

The originator of this recipe was preparing ravioli filling in the kitchen when some freshly caught flounder fillets arrived at the front door—resulting in the creation of this serendipitous new dish.

1 (10-ounce) package frozen
    chopped spinach, thawed,
    drained
¹/₂ cup lightly toasted bread
    crumbs
¹/₄ cup grated Romano cheese
¹/₄ cup grated Parmesan cheese

¹/₂ teaspoon basil
2 tablespoons finely chopped
    parsley
¹/₂ teaspoon minced garlic
milk
6 flounder fillets
Marinara Sauce

Combine the spinach, bread crumbs, Romano cheese, Parmesan cheese, basil, parsley and garlic in a bowl and mix well. Stir in enough milk to make a semi-stiff paste. Spread on 1 side of the flounder fillets. Roll up the fillets and secure with wooden picks. Place seam side down in a baking dish sprayed with olive oil cooking spray. Bake at 375 degrees for 30 minutes. Remove to a serving plate. Spoon Marinara Sauce over the fillets. Serve with angel hair pasta. Serve any extra sauce over the pasta.

Yield: 6 servings

Marinara Sauce

1 tablespoon minced garlic
2 tablespoons olive oil
3 (16-ounce) cans crushed
    tomatoes

1 (6-ounce) can tomato paste
1 teaspoon chopped oregano
1 teaspoon chopped parsley

Sauté the garlic in the olive oil in a saucepan. Stir in the undrained tomatoes, tomato paste, oregano and parsley. Bring to a boil; reduce the heat. Simmer for 15 minutes or until the mixture is heated through, stirring occasionally.

Yield: 4 to 5 cups

Farfalle Rivazza

clarified butter (see Editor's Note,
    page 126)
4 ounces prosciutto, chopped
4 cloves of garlic, minced
4 ounces onions, minced
³/₄ cup whipping cream

¹/₄ cup tomato sauce
salt and pepper to taste
¹/₄ cup grated Romano cheese
1 pound farfalle pasta, cooked,
    drained
vodka (optional)

Heat a skillet over high heat. Add clarified butter and prosciutto. Sauté until the prosciutto is crisp. Add the garlic and onions. Sauté until the onions are tender.

Add the whipping cream to the prosciutto mixture. Reduce the heat until the mixture simmers. Add the tomato sauce, salt and pepper. Cook until the mixture is somewhat reduced and thickened, stirring frequently. Stir in the cheese. Add the pasta and toss to mix. Remove from the heat. Add a small amount of vodka and flambé if desired.

Yield: 4 servings

from Chef Michael Owen of Trattoria Rivazza

Stuffed Roast Veal with Spinach

1 slice white bread
milk
12 ounces spinach, cooked, drained
4 ounces ground pork
4 ounces ground beef
2 ounces bacon or prosciutto, chopped
2 to 3 sprigs of parsley
2 eggs
3/4 cup grated Parmesan cheese
salt and pepper to taste

nutmeg to taste
1 large boned breast of veal
olive oil
1 rib celery, chopped
1 small onion, chopped
3 cloves of garlic, chopped
1 sprig of rosemary
1 sprig of sage
2 tablespoons butter
6 tablespoons dry white wine
6 tablespoons cold beef stock
1/2 teaspoon cornstarch

For the filling, soak the bread in milk to cover; drain well and tear into pieces. Squeeze the moisture from the spinach. Combine the spinach, ground pork, ground beef, bacon, bread pieces, parsley, eggs and cheese in a bowl and mix well. Season with salt, pepper and nutmeg.

Sprinkle the veal with salt. Spread the filling over the veal, leaving a 1/2-inch margin. Roll up the veal and tie it in several places with kitchen string. Brush olive oil over the veal and place in a roasting pan. Add the celery, onion, garlic, rosemary and sage. Dot with the butter. Bake at 400 degrees for 1 1/2 hours, turning 4 times and basting with the wine. Remove from the oven. Place the veal on a serving plate.

For the gravy, skim most of the fat from the pan drippings. Stir in a mixture of the beef stock and cornstarch. Simmer for several minutes or until the gravy is thickened. Serve with the veal.

Yield: 8 to 10 servings

Seafood Fettuccini

(Fettuccini al Frutti di Mare)

1 tablespoon olive oil
1/4 teaspoon finely chopped garlic
2 medium to large shrimp,
    peeled, deveined
2 medium to large scallops
2 clams, scrubbed
3 or 4 mussels, scrubbed

1 Roma tomato, peeled, chopped
1/2 cup pinot grigio
1/4 cup clam broth or fish stock
4 ounces fettuccini, cooked
1 tablespoon unsalted butter
salt and freshly ground pepper to
    taste

Heat a sauté pan over high heat and add the olive oil and garlic. Add the shrimp, scallops, clams and mussels. Sauté until the shrimp turn pink and the clams and mussels open. Add the tomato and mix well. Remove the clams and mussels and keep warm.

Stir the wine into the sauté pan gradually, scraping up any browned bits. Add the clam broth. Add the hot pasta and butter and mix well. Season with salt and pepper.

To serve, spoon the pasta mixture into a large pasta bowl. Arrange the clams and mussels around the bowl. Garnish the pasta with 3 thinly sliced basil leaves.

Yield: 1 serving

from Chef Dominique Venetico of Il Pasticcio Restaurant

Fillet of Beef with Gorgonzola

1 tablespoon olive oil
1 shallot, finely chopped
1/2 cup merlot
1/2 cup beef stock
1/2 carrot, julienned
6 pearl onions
1 teaspoon olive oil

1 (5-ounce) beef tenderloin, trimmed
salt and pepper to taste
2 tablespoons bread crumbs
1/4 ounce Gorgonzola cheese, crumbled
Polenta

For the sauce, heat 1 tablespoon olive oil in a saucepan. Add the shallot. Sauté until golden brown. Add the merlot and boil until reduced by 1/2. Add the beef stock and boil until reduced by 1/2. Set aside and keep warm.

To caramelize the carrot and onions, heat 1 teaspoon olive oil in a sauté pan. Add the carrot and onions. Sauté until dark golden brown. Set aside and keep warm.

Season the tenderloin on both sides with salt and pepper. Place on a rack in a roasting pan. Bake at 350 degrees until the meat has reached the desired degree of doneness. Process the bread crumbs and cheese in a food processor until mixed. Spread the mixture on the tenderloin. Return to the oven until the cheese is slightly melted.

To serve, place the caramelized mixture in the center of a serving plate. Place the tenderloin over the caramelized mixture. Spoon 1 tablespoon of the sauce over the top of the tenderloin. Garnish with an upright rosemary sprig. Place 1/4 cup of the polenta on opposite sides of the plate, reserving the remainder for another use. Serve with your favorite vegetables.

Yield: 1 serving

from Chef Dominique Venetico of Il Pasticcio Restaurant

Polenta

1 ounce Bel Paese cheese, shredded
1 ounce mozzarella cheese, shredded
1 ounce fontina cheese, shredded
1 ounce Gorgonzola cheese, shredded
1 (8-ounce) package polenta

Combine all the cheeses in a large bowl and mix well. Prepare the polenta using the package directions. Remove the polenta from the heat and stir in the cheese mixture with a wooden spoon.

Yield: 3 to 4 servings

Moussaka

2/3 cup bread crumbs

3 medium eggplant, peeled, sliced

salt to taste

3 large onions, chopped

olive oil

2 pounds ground lamb

3 tablespoons tomato paste

1/2 cup red wine

1/2 cup chopped parsley

1/4 teaspoon cinnamon

salt and pepper to taste

6 tablespoons butter

6 tablespoons flour

3 cups boiling milk

4 eggs, beaten

1/2 teaspoon nutmeg

1 (15-ounce) package ricotta
    cheese

1 cup freshly grated Parmesan
    cheese

Sprinkle a small amount of the bread crumbs in a greased 11x16-inch baking pan and set aside. Soak the eggplant in salted water for 15 minutes; drain well and squeeze the moisture from the eggplant. Spray the eggplant with olive oil cooking spray. Arrange the eggplant on a baking sheet and broil until lightly browned on both sides. Set aside.

For the meat sauce, sauté the onions in olive oil in a skillet until lightly browned. Add the lamb and sauté for 10 minutes or until no longer pink. Mix the tomato paste and wine in a bowl. Add the parsley, cinnamon, salt and pepper and mix well. Stir into the lamb mixture. Simmer over low heat until all the liquid has been absorbed. Remove from the heat and keep warm.

For the cream sauce, melt the butter in a saucepan. Add the flour gradually, whisking constantly. Add the milk gradually, whisking constantly. Cook until thickened and smooth, stirring constantly. Remove from the heat and let cool. Stir in the eggs, nutmeg and ricotta cheese.

Alternate layers of eggplant and meat sauce in the prepared baking pan, sprinkling each layer with Parmesan cheese. Top with the bread crumbs. Spoon the cream sauce over the top. Bake at 375 degrees until golden brown. Remove from the oven. Let cool for 20 minutes before cutting into squares. This dish is even better the second day.

Yield: 8 to 10 servings

Mushroom Tart

(Torta di Funghi)

³/₄ cup dried porcini mushrooms
¹/₂ cup apple cider
¹/₃ cup butter
¹/₄ cup olive oil
1 or 2 medium onions, chopped
8 ounces fresh mushrooms, sliced
¹/₂ cup chopped Italian parsley
1 clove of garlic, minced
1 shallot, minced
¹/₂ teaspoon dried oregano

¹/₄ teaspoon salt
¹/₄ teaspoon freshly ground
 pepper
1 tablespoon Cognac or sherry
1 (17-ounce) package puff pastry
2 eggs
1¹/₂ cups whipping cream
³/₄ cup shredded mozzarella
 cheese
¹/₄ cup grated Parmesan cheese

Soak the porcini mushrooms in the apple cider; drain well. Melt the butter in a large skillet and add the olive oil. Add the onions, fresh mushrooms, porcini mushrooms, parsley, garlic, shallot, oregano, salt and pepper. Sauté until the onions are translucent but not brown. Remove to a bowl and let cool. Chill, covered, overnight. Stir the Cognac into the mushroom mixture. Chill, covered, overnight.

Cut the puff pastry into strips. Place the strips in a 9-inch tart pan with a removable bottom. Press the strips lightly against the bottom and side of the pan; trim any excess pastry from around the rim. Cut a circle of parchment paper to fit the bottom of the pan. Place inside the crust and add pie weights or dried beans. Bake at 400 degrees for 15 minutes. Remove from the oven and let cool. Remove the parchment paper and pie weights.

Beat the eggs and whipping cream in a bowl with a whisk. Stir in the mozzarella cheese and Parmesan cheese. Add to the mushroom mixture and mix well. Spoon into the tart shell. Bake at 375 degrees for 30 minutes. Let cool for 5 minutes before cutting into wedges. Serve hot or at room temperature.

Yield: 4 to 6 servings

Escarole and White Beans

1 bunch escarole, trimmed,
    chopped
salt to taste
3 tablespoons olive oil
2 cloves of garlic, minced

$^1/_8$ teaspoon red pepper flakes
2 (19-ounce) cans white kidney
    beans, drained, rinsed
1 (10-ounce) can cream of celery
    soup

Cook the escarole in boiling salted water to cover in a saucepan for
5 minutes; drain well and set aside.

Heat the olive oil in a large skillet over low heat. Add the garlic and
red pepper flakes. Cook for 2 to 3 minutes or until the garlic is lightly
browned. Stir in the beans, soup and escarole. Cook over low heat for
30 minutes or until heated through, stirring occasionally. Season with
additional salt. Serve immediately.

Yield: 4 to 6 servings

Il Pasticcio's Crème Brûlée

5 egg yolks

¹/₂ cup sugar

2 cups whipping cream

2 tablespoons vanilla extract

4 teaspoons brown sugar

Combine the egg yolks and sugar in a bowl and whisk until the mixture is a creamy yellow. Set aside.

Combine the whipping cream and vanilla in a saucepan and whisk until mixed. Cook over medium heat until the mixture is steaming but not boiling. Remove from the heat. Stir a small amount of the hot cream mixture into the egg yolks; stir the egg yolks into the hot cream mixture. Cook over medium heat until the mixture is slightly thickened and coats the back of a spoon, stirring constantly.

Ladle ³/₄ cup of the cream mixture into each of 5 ramekins. Place the ramekins in a shallow baking pan. Add enough water to the baking pan to come halfway up the side of the ramekins. Bake at 250 degrees for 1 hour. Place the baking pan in a larger pan of ice and chill for 2 hours.

Place the ramekins on a baking sheet. Smooth brown sugar over each crème brûlée. Broil until the brown sugar is evenly caramelized. Serve plain or with your favorite fruit.

Yield: 5 servings

Cassata alla Siciliana

1 (9-inch) pound cake
16 ounces ricotta cheese
2 tablespoons whipping cream
$^{1}/_{2}$ cup sugar
3 tablespoons Grand Marnier

3 tablespoons coarsely chopped
   candied mixed fruit
2 ounces semisweet chocolate,
   coarsely chopped
Chocolate Frosting

Slice the end crusts off the pound cake and level the top. Cut the cake horizontally into $^{1}/_{2}$- to $^{3}/_{4}$-inch layers. For the filling, press the ricotta cheese through a sieve into a mixer bowl and beat until smooth. Add the whipping cream, sugar and Grand Marnier, beating constantly. Fold in the mixed fruit and chocolate.

    Place 1 cake layer on a flat plate and spread with the filling. Repeat the layers until all the filling has been used and 1 cake layer remains. Top with the remaining cake layer. Press the layers together gently. Chill for 2 hours or until firm. Spread Chocolate Frosting over the top and sides of the dessert. Chill, covered loosely with plastic wrap, for 24 hours or longer.

Yield: 8 servings

Chocolate Frosting

12 ounces semisweet chocolate,
   chopped
$^{3}/_{4}$ cup strong black coffee

1 cup cold unsalted butter, cut
   into small pieces

Combine the chocolate and coffee in a saucepan. Cook over low heat until the chocolate is melted, stirring constantly. Remove from the heat. Beat in the butter 1 piece at a time until smooth. Chill until of a spreadable consistency.

Yield: 1 $^{1}/_{2}$ to 2 cups

Frozen Cassata

1 cup chopped cherries
¹/₂ cup maraschino or orange
   liqueur
1²/₃ cups sugar
¹/₂ cup water
6 egg whites
1³/₄ cups coarsely chopped
   walnuts

1 quart whipping cream,
   whipped
¹/₂ gallon vanilla ice cream
1 large sponge cake, sliced
¹/₂ gallon raspberry ice

Mix the cherries and liqueur in a bowl and set aside. Bring the sugar and
water to a boil in a saucepan. Let cool until the mixture reaches 236 degrees
on a candy thermometer, soft-ball stage. Beat the egg whites in a mixer bowl
until stiff peaks form. Add the hot sugar mixture in a steady stream, beating
constantly until soft peaks form. Set the bowl into ice water to cool the
mixture. Add the cooled syrup and walnuts to the cherry mixture. Fold in
the whipped cream.

Layer half the ice cream, sponge cake and raspberry ice in each of two
5x9-inch loaf pans. Top with the cherry mixture. Freeze until firm.

Yield: 16 servings

Gala Affairs

Opening night of the Savannah Symphony Orchestra's Masterworks
Series is a gala event. The first concert of the season is preceded by a
catered black-tie dinner at one of the Civic Center's banquet rooms.
Floral arrangements are provided by members of the Guild. Antique
jewelry adorns the gowns of the ladies in attendance.

Those who prefer to entertain at home on opening night may select
a menu that is delicious but light, keeping in mind the musical treats
that lie ahead: Schumann's Symphony No. 3 in E-flat major, "Rhenish,"
and Brahms' Piano Concerto No. 1 in D minor with Ruth Laredo as
the featured performer in the first concert of a recent season.

A black-tie cocktail buffet at a historic home in downtown Savannah
or a low-country mansion on the Vernon River will draw a waiting list
for the PARTIES A LA CARTE committee. A bourbon on the rocks or
a glass of chardonnay may be followed by crab cakes or sliced
sugar-cured ham. A full moon over the marsh and Emma Kelly on
the piano, tinkling out the notes of "As Time Goes By," add nostalgia
and romance to the evening.

LeVow '98

Contents

Menu

Elizabeth's Overture

Oyster and Spinach Bisque
(page 154)

Grilled Tuna with Saffron Sauce and Mango Salsa
(page 164)

Spiced Beef Tenderloin
(page 155)

Green Peppercorn Madeira Sauce
(page 155)

Asparagus with Country Ham (page 156)

Cheese and fruit assortment

White Chocolate Mousse
(page 157)

Crisp Sliced Potatoes

6 medium baking potatoes
6 tablespoons melted butter
kosher salt to taste

Peel the potatoes and place in a bowl of cold water until needed. Cut ¼ inch off each end and 1 side of 1 potato so that it will handle easily on the cutting board. Cut the potato lengthwise into 12 thin slices, holding the slices together. Place the blade of the knife under the potato and lift onto a buttered baking sheet. Push with the palm of the hand to flatten and fan the potato. Brush with melted butter. Repeat with the remaining potatoes. Bake at 350 degrees in the top third of the oven for 40 minutes or until the potatoes are tender on the inside and crisp and golden brown on the outside. Sprinkle with kosher salt.

Yield: 6 servings

Oyster and Spinach Bisque

2 pints small fresh oysters with their liquor
chicken broth
2 cups cubed peeled potatoes
½ cup cubed Vidalia onion or Spanish onion
½ cup sliced leeks
¼ cup minced white celery
1 teaspoon minced garlic
2 bay leaves

2 tablespoons butter
1 cup water
1 cup chicken broth
½ cup dry white vermouth or dry white wine
1 cup half-and-half
1 teaspoon hot pepper sauce
½ teaspoon salt
1 cup julienned fresh spinach
2 tablespoons minced fresh chives

Check the oysters for shells. Add enough chicken broth to the oyster liquor to measure 2 cups. Set aside.

Combine the potatoes, onion, leeks, celery, garlic, bay leaves, butter, water and 1 cup chicken broth in a large stockpot and mix well. Simmer, covered, over medium heat for 10 minutes or until the flavors have blended. Do not brown the vegetables at this stage; reduce the heat if necessary. Add the oyster liquor mixture and the vermouth and mix gently. Simmer, covered, for 15 minutes or until the potatoes are very tender. Remove and discard the bay leaves. Add the half-and-half, hot pepper sauce and salt to the bisque and mix gently.

Heat the oysters in a saucepan until the edges curl. Stir the oysters and any pan drippings into the bisque. Stir in the spinach. Ladle the bisque into bowls to serve. Sprinkle each serving with chives.

Yield: 6 servings

Spiced Beef Tenderloin

1 teaspoon ground cinnamon
1 tablespoon each ground
    coriander, pepper, allspice
    and cumin
1 tablespoon kosher salt

2 tablespoons olive oil
2 tablespoons melted butter
1 (2¹/₂-pound) beef tenderloin,
    trimmed

Mix the cinnamon, coriander, pepper, allspice, cumin and salt in a bowl. Add the olive oil and melted butter and mix well. Rub on all sides of the tenderloin. Marinate, covered, in the refrigerator for 30 minutes. Remove the tenderloin from the marinade, discarding the remaining marinade. Place the tenderloin on a rack in a baking pan. Bake at 375 degrees for 35 minutes or until medium-rare. Remove from the oven and let stand for 5 minutes. To serve chilled, wrap the tenderloin in foil and freeze for 30 minutes. Remove to the refrigerator until ready to slice. Serve with Green Peppercorn Madeira Sauce.

Yield: 6 servings

Green Peppercorn Madeira Sauce

1 tablespoon virgin olive oil
1 teaspoon minced garlic
1 teaspoon minced shallot
¹/₄ cup madeira
1 teaspoon grated lemon peel

1 tablespoon lemon juice
¹/₄ cup whipping cream
2 tablespoons green peppercorns
6 tablespoons cold unsalted
    butter, cut into cubes

Combine the olive oil, garlic, shallot, madeira, lemon peel and lemon juice in a small sauté pan. Simmer over high heat until reduced to 2 tablespoons. Stir in the whipping cream and peppercorns. Simmer until reduced to 4 tablespoons. Reduce the heat to medium. Add the butter 1 piece at a time, whisking constantly until the butter is melted and the sauce is thick. Strain the sauce and keep warm to prevent the sauce from separating. You can use a thermos for this or set the sauce over a pan of hot water for up to 2 hours.

Yield: ¹/₂ cup

Asparagus with Country Ham

2 tablespoons olive oil
1 cup minced country ham
2 cups minced leeks, rinsed twice
48 thin stalks of fresh asparagus,
    trimmed, rinsed

1/4 cup water
Lemon Butter Sauce
1/2 cup toasted sliced almonds

Combine the olive oil, ham and leeks in a large skillet. Sauté over high heat until the ham and leeks are lightly browned. Add the asparagus and water and mix well. Simmer, covered, for 3 minutes or until the asparagus is tender. The water will evaporate but do not let the asparagus brown. Remove the asparagus to a serving platter with a slotted spoon. Spoon the ham mixture over the asparagus. Top with Lemon Butter Sauce and toasted almonds.

Yield: 6 servings

Lemon Butter Sauce

1 tablespoon virgin olive oil
1 teaspoon minced garlic
1 teaspoon minced shallot
    (optional)
1/4 cup white wine or dry white
    vermouth

1 teaspoon minced grated lemon
    peel
1 tablespoon lemon juice
1/4 cup whipping cream
6 tablespoons cold unsalted
    butter, cut into cubes

Combine the olive oil, garlic, shallot, wine, lemon peel and lemon juice in a small sauté pan. Simmer over high heat until reduced to about 2 tablespoons. Stir in the whipping cream. Simmer until reduced to about 4 tablespoons (this will happen quickly). Reduce the heat to medium. Add the butter 1 piece at a time, whisking constantly until all the butter is melted and the sauce is thick (this will happen quickly). Strain the sauce and keep warm to prevent the sauce from separating.

Yield: 1/2 cup

White Chocolate Mousse

1 cup whipping cream
1 teaspoon crème de cacao
1¹/₂ teaspoons unflavored gelatin

¹/₂ cup whipping cream
4 ounces white chocolate,
    chopped

Beat 1 cup whipping cream and crème de cacao in a mixer bowl until soft peaks form. Chill until needed. Sprinkle the gelatin over ¹/₂ cup whipping cream in a small saucepan. Let stand for 2 minutes or until softened. Cook over medium heat until hot but not boiling, stirring until the gelatin is dissolved. Place the white chocolate in a food processor container and add the hot cream mixture. Process until the white chocolate is melted and smooth. Let stand for 1 to 2 minutes or until the white chocolate is cool but not firm. Fold the white chocolate into the chilled whipped cream. Spoon into 8 individual mousse cups. Top with Raspberry Purée.

Yield: 8 servings

Raspberry Purée

1 pint fresh raspberries
2 tablespoons water
¹/₃ cup sugar

2 tablespoons Grand Marnier or
    other orange-flavored liqueur

Place the raspberries in a food processor container. Combine the water and sugar in a small saucepan. Cook over low heat, stirring until the sugar is dissolved. Stir in the Grand Marnier. Pour over the raspberries and process until puréed. Strain if desired.

Yield: 2¹/₂ cups

Crab Tassies

½ cup butter, softened
3 ounces cream cheese, softened
1 cup flour
¼ teaspoon salt
1 pound crab meat, flaked
½ cup mayonnaise
1 tablespoon lemon juice
¼ cup finely chopped celery

2 small scallions, finely chopped
½ cup shredded Swiss cheese
½ teaspoon Worcestershire sauce
¼ teaspoon seasoned salt
dash of Tabasco sauce
fresh dillweed to taste (optional)
1 teaspoon sherry (optional)

For the baking shells, cream the butter and cream cheese in a mixer bowl until light and fluffy. Stir in the flour and salt. Shape into 24 small balls. Chill for 1 hour. Press the balls into small nonstick muffin cups. For the filling, combine the crab meat, mayonnaise, lemon juice, celery, scallions, cheese, Worcestershire sauce, seasoned salt, Tabasco sauce, dillweed and sherry in a bowl and mix well. Spoon into the shells. Bake at 350 degrees for 30 minutes or until golden brown. Add color by sprinkling the tassies very lightly with paprika before baking if desired.

Yield: 24 servings

Roquefort Grapes

1 cup walnuts or pecans
2 to 3 ounces Roquefort cheese or
   Danish bleu cheese, crumbled

8 ounces cream cheese, softened
1 pound seedless grapes, rinsed,
   dried

Spread the walnuts on a baking sheet. Bake at 275 degrees until light golden brown. Chop the walnuts and spread on a plate. Mix the Roquefort cheese and cream cheese in a food processor. Place the cheese mixture on a plate. Roll the grapes in the cheese mixture, then in the walnuts. Place the grapes on a waxed paper-lined tray. Chill until serving time.

Yield: 10 to 15 servings

Oysters with Leek Fondue

24 oysters on the half shell
1 cup Champagne or dry white
 wine

Leek Fondue
2 tablespoons chopped chives

Remove the oysters from the shell and wash the shells. Poach the oysters in the Champagne in a skillet for 1 minute or just until the edges curl; drain well. Place 1 oyster in each shell and top with about 1 tablespoon of the Leek Fondue. Sprinkle with chives and serve immediately.

Yield: 4 servings

Leek Fondue

2 cups unsalted butter
2 cups julienned leeks

1 cup water
salt and pepper to taste

Cut the butter into tablespoon-sized pieces. Combine the leeks and water in a saucepan. Boil, covered, for 15 minutes or until tender. Boil, uncovered, until the liquid is reduced to 1/4 cup. Add the butter 1 piece at a time, whisking constantly until smooth and creamy. Season with salt and pepper.

Yield: 2 to 3 cups

from Chef Walter Dasher of the Chatham Club

Cocktail Time Pickled Shrimp

1½ pounds shrimp, boiled,
    peeled, deveined
2 medium onions, thinly sliced
1¼ cups vegetable oil
¾ cup cider vinegar

1 teaspoon salt
1 teaspoon Worcestershire sauce
2 teaspoons capers
2 teaspoons celery seeds
1 teaspoon Tabasco sauce

Layer the shrimp and onion slices alternately in a large bowl. Mix the oil, vinegar, salt, Worcestershire sauce, capers, celery seeds and Tabasco sauce in a medium bowl and pour over the shrimp and onion slices. Chill, tightly covered, for 2 to 3 days.

Yield: 12 servings

Pâté en Croûte

8 ounces liverwurst
2 eggs, hard-cooked
½ cup shredded Edam cheese
¼ cup Dijon mustard

¼ cup mayonnaise
1 teaspoon Worcestershire sauce
¼ cup chopped scallions
2 (12-inch) loaves French bread

For the pâté, combine the liverwurst, eggs, cheese, Dijon mustard, mayonnaise, Worcestershire sauce and scallions in a food processor container and process until mixed. For the crust, cut the ends from each bread loaf. Cut each loaf into 3 or 4 pieces. Scoop out the center of the pieces and fill with pâté. Chill, wrapped individually in plastic wrap, overnight. Cut into slices to serve.

Yield: 12 servings

Butternut Squash Soup

1 medium white onion, peeled,
  chopped
3 butternut squash, peeled,
  chopped
1/2 cup butter
2 Granny Smith apples, peeled,
  chopped
1/2 gallon chicken stock
2 cups whipping cream
salt and pepper to taste

Cook the onion in the butter in a saucepan until tender but not browned. Add the squash and apples and mix well. Add the chicken stock. Cook until the apples are tender. Cool slightly. Purée in a blender. Return the puréed mixture to the saucepan. Cook until heated through. Fold in the whipping cream. Cook until heated through. Season with salt and pepper. Garnish each serving with maple-flavored whipped cream sprinkled with cinnamon.

Yield: 8 to 10 servings

from Chef Debra Reid Noelk of 17 Hundred 90 Restaurant

Mrs. Bannon's Crab Stew

2 ribs celery, finely chopped
1 unpeeled lemon, chopped, seeded
3 tablespoons butter
2 tablespoons flour
1 (12-ounce) can evaporated milk
1 (5-ounce) can evaporated milk
2 cups plus 6 tablespoons milk
salt and cayenne pepper to taste
2 hard-cooked eggs, chopped
1 pound crab claw meat, flaked
Worcestershire sauce to taste
1/2 cup sherry, heated

Boil the celery and lemon in a small amount of water in a saucepan until most of the liquid has evaporated; keep warm. Melt the butter in a heavy 4-quart saucepan. Stir in the flour gradually. Stir in the evaporated milk and milk gradually. Season with salt and cayenne pepper. Add the celery mixture, eggs and crab meat and mix well. Stir in Worcestershire sauce and sherry.

Yield: 6 to 7 servings

Mrs. Bannon ran a lodge at Thunderbolt, a small fishing community on the Wilmington River near Savannah. Her crab stew was worth the drive from town.

Geechee Herb-Stuffed Shad and Roe

1 cup minced celery
1 cup chopped onion
1/3 cup chopped green or red bell
    pepper
1/4 cup butter
1 teaspoon tarragon
1/2 teaspoon summer savory
1/2 teaspoon poultry seasoning
1/2 teaspoon herbes de Provence
    (optional)

6 slices bread, toasted, torn into
    pieces
1 tablespoon chopped parsley
salt and pepper to taste
2 (1-pound) shad fillets
paprika to taste
1/4 cup melted butter
juice of 1/2 lemon
1 pair of roe (roe from 1 shad)

Combine the celery, onion, green pepper and 1/4 cup butter in a skillet. Cook until the vegetables are tender and browned, stirring frequently. Add the tarragon, summer savory, poultry seasoning, herbes de Provence, bread pieces, parsley, salt and pepper. Add hot water a few spoonfuls at a time until the mixture is the consistency of stuffing, stirring frequently. Remove from the heat and keep warm.

Place 1 shad fillet on a greased ovenproof serving platter and cover with the stuffing. Top with the remaining fillet. Sprinkle with paprika and drizzle with the melted butter and lemon juice. Bake at 350 degrees for 45 to 60 minutes or until the fish flakes easily, adding the roe alongside the shad 25 minutes before the end of the baking time. The roe should be salted, peppered and turned after 10 minutes. Baste the shad and roe occasionally throughout the entire baking time.

Yield: 5 servings

Although fairly common along the Atlantic Coast, shad from the Ogeechee River, boned by experts like those at Russo's Seafood, makes for a special dish.

Beef Tenderloin on Arugula

olive oil
1 (2-pound) beef tenderloin
salt and freshly ground pepper to
    taste
4 cups arugula, trimmed

$^1/_2$ cup shaved celery
4 ounces Parmesan cheese,
    shaved very thin
Tomato Vinaigrette

Drizzle olive oil into a hot skillet. Add the tenderloin when the olive oil begins to smoke. Cook until seared on both sides. Season lightly with salt and pepper. Cook for 5 minutes or to desired degree of doneness, turning once. Remove the meat from the skillet and slice thinly.

Arrange the arugula on a serving plate and top with the beef slices. Sprinkle the celery and cheese over the beef. Drizzle with Tomato Vinaigrette. Serve hot or cold.

Yield: 4 servings

Tomato Vinaigrette

$^1/_2$ cup extra-virgin olive oil
$^1/_2$ cup lemon juice
1 plum tomato, chopped
$^1/_2$ cup fresh basil

1 jalapeño, chopped (optional)
2 cloves of garlic, chopped
salt and freshly ground pepper to
    taste

Combine the olive oil, lemon juice, tomato, basil, jalapeño, garlic, salt and pepper in a blender container and process until very smooth and thick.

Yield: 1$^3/_4$ to 2 cups

from Chef/Owner Suzy Massetti of Zanzare Ristorante

Mango Salsa

1 semi-ripe mango, cut into
cubes
1 jalapeño, seeded, cut into
small cubes
1/3 red bell pepper, cut into
small cubes
2 tablespoons chopped
cilantro
2 tablespoons chopped
shallots
juice of 1 small lemon

Combine the mango, jalapeño,
red pepper, cilantro and shallots
in a small bowl and mix well.
Stir in the lemon juice.

Yield: 1 to 1 1/2 cups

Grilled Tuna with Saffron Sauce and Mango Salsa

1 1/2 pounds yellowfin tuna   Saffron Sauce
salt and pepper to taste   Mango Salsa
vegetable oil

Season the tuna lightly with salt and pepper and brush with oil. Grill for 3
minutes per side or until medium rare. Spoon Saffron Sauce onto a serving
platter. Place the tuna over the sauce. Spoon Mango Salsa over the tuna.
The tuna may be seared in a nonstick skillet instead of being grilled.

Yield: 4 servings

Saffron Sauce

1/4 cup white wine   pinch of saffron threads
1 tablespoon lemon juice   1/2 cup butter, at room
2 tablespoons chopped shallots   temperature

Combine the wine, lemon juice, shallots and saffron in an 8-inch saucepan.
Cook over medium heat until the liquid is reduced to 2 tablespoons. Whisk
in the butter.

Yield: 1/2 to 3/4 cup

from Chef Dan Kim of the Olde Pink House Restaurant

Potato Latkes

4 potatoes, cut into 2-inch cubes
1 onion, chopped
2 eggs
1 teaspoon salt

pinch of pepper
1/4 cup flour
2 teaspoons baking powder
vegetable oil

Process the potatoes, onion, eggs, salt, pepper, flour and baking powder in a food processor until the potatoes are finely chopped. Heat oil in a cast-iron skillet. Drop the potato mixture by tablespoonfuls into the hot oil. Cook each batch until browned on both sides, turning once. Remove and keep warm. Serve with homemade chunky applesauce and/or sour cream.

Yield: 8 servings

Sweet Potatoes with Cointreau

1 (11-ounce) can mandarin
   oranges
2 (16-ounce) cans sweet potatoes,
   drained
1 (8-ounce) can sliced water
   chestnuts

2 apples, peeled, cut into cubes
3 tablespoons butter
1/2 cup sugar
1/4 cup Cointreau
2 teaspoons cinnamon
2 teaspoons ginger

Drain the mandarin oranges, reserving the juice. Mash the sweet potatoes in a bowl. Add the mandarin oranges, water chestnuts and apples and mix well. Combine the reserved orange juice, butter, sugar, Cointreau, cinnamon and ginger in a double boiler. Cook until syrupy, stirring frequently. Stir the syrup into the sweet potato mixture. Spoon into a buttered casserole. Bake, covered, at 350 degrees for 45 minutes.

Yield: 8 to 10 servings

Potato latkes are a traditional Hanukkah dish, but Martha Stewart makes a smaller version to serve with sour cream and caviar for hors d'oeuvre.

165

Barley and Mushroom Casserole

6 tablespoons butter
2 cloves of garlic, minced
2 yellow onions, minced
1 pound mushrooms, thinly
    sliced
1 cup pearl barley

¹/₂ tablespoon dried basil
3 cups chicken stock
salt and freshly ground pepper
    to taste
¹/₄ cup chopped parsley

Melt the butter in a 2-quart Dutch oven. Add the garlic and onions. Sauté over medium-low heat for 5 minutes or until the onions are translucent. Add the mushrooms. Sauté for 5 minutes or until the mushrooms are golden brown. Add the pearl barley and basil and toss lightly. Add the chicken stock and mix well. Season with salt and pepper. Bring to a boil and remove from the heat. Bake, covered, at 375 degrees for 45 to 50 minutes or until the barley is tender. Add the parsley just before serving and toss gently. Serve hot. This recipe can be halved.

Yield: 6 to 8 servings

Ricotta Zucchini

1 small onion, chopped
8 ounces zucchini, chopped
¹/₂ teaspoon butter
3 tablespoons flour
dash of salt and pepper
¹/₂ teaspoon dried basil

3 eggs
1 (15-ounce) package ricotta
    cheese
¹/₂ cup shredded Cheddar cheese
dash of nutmeg

Sauté the onion and zucchini in the butter in a skillet. Stir in the flour, salt, pepper and basil. Remove from the heat. Add the eggs, ricotta cheese, Cheddar cheese and nutmeg and mix well. Spoon into a 1¹/₂-quart casserole. Bake at 375 degrees for 40 to 45 minutes or until heated through.

Yield: 4 to 6 servings

Cheesecake Anno

1 cup sifted flour
1/4 cup sugar
1 teaspoon grated lemon peel
1 teaspoon vanilla extract
1 egg yolk
1/2 cup butter, softened
2 1/2 pounds cream cheese, softened

1 3/4 cups sugar
3 tablespoons flour
1 1/2 teaspoons grated lemon peel
1 tablespoon lemon juice
1 teaspoon vanilla extract
5 eggs
2 egg yolks
1/2 cup whipping cream

For the crust, combine 1 cup flour, 1/4 cup sugar, 1 teaspoon lemon peel and 1 teaspoon vanilla in a bowl and mix well. Add 1 egg yolk and butter and mix until a soft dough forms. Chill, wrapped in waxed paper, for 30 to 60 minutes. Break off 1/3 of the dough and press onto the bottom of a 9-inch springform pan. Bake at 400 degrees for 10 minutes or until very lightly browned. Place on a wire rack to cool. Increase the oven temperature to 550 degrees. Pat the remaining dough onto the sides of the springform pan, sealing the dough to the baked crust.

For the filling, combine the cream cheese, 1 3/4 cups sugar, 3 tablespoons flour, 1 1/2 teaspoons lemon peel, lemon juice and 1 teaspoon vanilla in a mixer bowl and blend well. Add 5 eggs and 2 egg yolks 1 at a time, beating lightly after each addition. Blend in the whipping cream. Spoon into the springform pan.

Bake for 12 minutes. Reduce the oven temperature to 250 degrees. Bake for 1 hour. Chill for 5 hours to overnight before serving. The cheesecake may be frozen after chilling; bring to room temperature before serving.

Yield: 10 servings

This recipe from the Atlanta restaurant Anno won the Best Cheesecake in Atlanta Award in the early 1980s.

Blueberry Cobbler with Brandy Vanilla Sauce

1 cup butter
2 cups sugar
1¹/₂ cups flour
4 teaspoons baking powder

¹/₂ teaspoon salt
1¹/₂ cups milk
2 cups blueberries
Brandy Vanilla Sauce

Melt the butter in a 9x11-inch baking dish. Combine the sugar, flour, baking powder, salt and milk in a bowl and mix well. Pour over the melted butter in the baking dish. Spoon the blueberries over the flour mixture. Bake at 350 degrees for 25 minutes or until golden brown. Pour Brandy Vanilla Sauce over the cobbler. Garnish each serving with sliced fruit or berries.

Yield: 6 to 12 servings

Brandy Vanilla Sauce

¹/₂ teaspoon butter
¹/₄ cup brandy
2 tablespoons vanilla extract

¹/₂ cup whipping cream
3 tablespoons sugar

Melt the butter in a sauté pan. Add the brandy, vanilla, whipping cream and sugar and mix well. Boil until the sauce is reduced by ¹/₂.

Yield: 12 to 14 tablespoons

from 3-2-1 Café's Chef Michael Provani

Fresh Apple Cake

3 cups chopped apples
2 cups sugar
1 1/2 cups vegetable oil
3 eggs, beaten
1 teaspoon baking soda

1 teaspoon salt
3 cups sifted flour
2 teaspoons vanilla extract
Caramel Icing

Combine the apples, sugar and oil in a bowl and mix well. Add the eggs, baking soda, salt, flour and vanilla and mix well. Spoon into a greased 9x13-inch cake pan. Place in a cold oven and set the temperature at 325 degrees. Bake for 1 hour. Pierce the top of the hot cake several times with a fork. Spoon Caramel Icing over the top, allowing the icing to soak into the cake. Let cool before cutting into squares.

Yield: 15 to 18 servings

Caramel Icing

1 cup packed light brown sugar
1/2 cup butter

1/4 cup sweetened condensed milk
1 teaspoon vanilla extract

Combine the brown sugar, butter and condensed milk in a saucepan. Bring to a slow boil and remove from the heat. Stir in the vanilla.

Yield: 1 3/4 cups

Contributors

Anita Alkofer
Elizabeth Anderson
Libba Anderson
Paula Badalamenti
Geoffrey Batton, Owner, Sapphire Grill
André Baxter, Chef, The Tea Room Restaurant
Bella's Italian Cafe, Joyce Shanks
Arlene Belzer
Bodi's, Richard Halperin
Bodi's, Alfreda Payne, Chef
Carole Boudinot
Roslyn Brown
Dian Brownfield
Robert Bryan, Executive Chef, The River's End Restaurant
Esther Buchsbaum
Marty Buckingham
Mark R. Burns, Chef, Huey's Restaurant
Anne Carpenter
Mary Alice Cavitt
Scott Center
Samuel L. Chandler, Jr.,
        Hunter Horn Plantation Hams
Chatham Club, Walter Dasher, Chef
Julia Cohen, The Preferred Caterers, Atlanta
Marion Conlin
Patti Cooper
Creative Catering, John Menzies
Ida L. Dalziel
Walter Dasher, Chef, Chatham Club
Lynne H. Davis
Sandra Edgar Davis
Iris Dayoub
DeSoto Hilton Hotel, Cedric Vanterpool, Executive Chef
Lu Downs
Penny Dulaney
Danyse G. Edel
Elizabeth on Thirty Seventh, Elizabeth Terry, Chef
Nele Ewaldsen
First City Club, Peter Schott, Chef
45 South Restaurant, Joseph Lemos, Chef

Joan E. Gefen
A. M. Goldkrand
Mary Ann Gonis
Philip Greenberg, Maestro, Savannah Symphony
Shannon Greenberg
W. Scott Grimmitt, Chef, Season's Restaurant
Richard Halperin, Sophisticated Palate/Bodi's
E. Peaches Harbourne
Frank Harris, River House Seafood Restaurant
Jo Hedley
Norman Heidt, Johnny Harris Restaurant
Mary Ann Hess
Maureen Horvath
Huey's Restaurant, Mark R. Burns, Chef
Hunter Horn Plantation Hams, Samuel L. Chandler, Jr.
Il Pasticcio Restaurant, Dominique Venetico, Chef
Marianne Innes
John Jawback, Chef, Jean Louise Restaurant
Jean Louise Restaurant, John Jawback, Chef
Alice Jepson
Johnny Harris Restaurant, Norman Heidt
Betty Johnson
Chris Johnson
Jane Kahn
Dan Kim, Chef, Olde Pink House Restaurant
Anne Krahl
Bailee Kronowitz
Nancy J. Larsen
Katie Lemasters
Joseph Lemos, Chef, 45 South Restaurant
Kathy Levitt
Fran Levow
Joan Levy
Margie Levy
Ellen Lew, Caterer
Marina Lindblom
Ann Register Link
Dottie Lynch
Laura Belle Macrae
Susan Mason, Caterer

Suzy Massetti, Chef/Owner, Zanzare Ristorante
Debby Maule
Ann McGraw
Susan McKowen
Barbara McLaughlin
Marion L. Mendel
John Menzies, Creative Catering
Grace Lyon Merritt
Joanne Merritt
Linda Miller
Nancy Mitchell
Marion Moore
Mary Murray
Chris Nason, Chef, Sapphire Grill
Anna Nichols
Debra Reid Noelk, Chef, 17 Hundred 90 Restaurant
Betty Norman
Olde Pink House Restaurant, Dan Kim, Chef
Sonia C. Oram
Marolyn Overton
Michael Owen, Chef, Trattoria Rivazza
Susan Palmer
Jeanne Papy
Alfreda Payne, Chef, Sophisticated Palate/Bodi's
Preferred Caterers, Atlanta, Julia Cohen
Leslie Preston
Michael Provani, Chef/Owner, 3-2-1 Cafe
Mary Helen Ray
Suzanne M. Reid
Bonnie Retsas, Chef/Owner, Soho South Cafe
Evelyne Rioux-Moore
River House Seafood Restaurant, Frank Harris
River's End Restaurant, Robert Bryan, Executive Chef
Dede Roberts
Joan Robinson
Midge Rossini
Vincent Russo, Caterer
Cheryl Sanders
Sapphire Grill, Geoffrey Batton, Owner
Sapphire Grill, Chris Nason, Chef

Savannah Symphony, Philip Greenberg, Maestro
Peter Schott, Chef, First City Club
Season's Restaurant, W. Scott Grimmitt, Chef
Pat Seguare
17 Hundred 90 Restaurant, Debra Reid Noelk, Chef
Joyce Shanks, Bella's Italian Cafe
Esther Shaver
Hope Sherry
Betty W. Siler
Barbara O. Smith
Jack Smith
Soho South Cafe, Bonnie Retsas, Chef/Owner
Sophisticated Palate, Richard Halperin
Sophisticated Palate, Alfreda Payne, Chef
Willa Steinhauser
Ruth Stuenckel
Angela C. Su
Elizabeth Terry, Chef, Elizabeth on Thirty Seventh
The Tea Room, Andre Baxter, Chef
3-2-1 Cafe, Michael Provani, Chef/Owner
Erlinda G. Torres
Trattoria Rivazza, Michael Owen, Chef
Joey Trescott
Ellie Trumbore
Jane Van Gigch
Catherine Van Valkenburg
Cedric Vanterpool, Executive Chef, DeSoto Hilton Hotel
Dominique Venetico, Chef, Il Pasticcio Restaurant
Marguerite Warfield
C. Don Waters
Nancy Wheeler
Marie L. White
Mary Lou Williams
Rose Ann Williams
Janet Wilson
Pris Wilson
Marion Worthy
Faye Wray
Pamela Young
Zanzare Ristorante, Suzy Massetti, Chef/Owner

171

Index

Tuna
Grilled Tuna with Saffron Sauce and
Mango Salsa, 164
Spanish Fishermen's Rice
Salad, 93
Tuna Sauce, 16

Veal
Country Braised Veal Shanks with
Carrots, 67

Osso Buco with Sherry, Cognac and
Marsala, 32
Stuffed Roast Veal with Spinach, 141
Vitello Tonnato, 16

Vegetables. *See also* names of
vegetables
Asparagus with Country
Ham, 156
Chiles Rellenos, 87

Farfalle with Three Cheeses, Pancetta,
Tomatoes and Baby Peas, 131
Ginger Garlic Stir-Fried Vegetables, 111
Honey-Glazed Shallots, 67
Maque Choux, 50

Zucchini
Bread Salad, 134
Ricotta Zucchini, 166
Roasted Vegetable Minestrone, 138

Savannah à la Carte

Savannah Symphony Women's Guild

P.O. Box 9505 • Savannah, Georgia 31412-9505

Please send me _____ copies of *Savannah à la Carte* . . . . $24.95 each $ _____

Shipping. . . . . 3.50 each $ _____

Sales Tax (Georgia residents only) . . . . 1.95 each $ _____

Total Enclosed $ _____

Name

Address

City   State   Zip

Daytime Phone (   )

Method of Payment: [   ] VISA   [   ] MasterCard
[   ] Check or Money Order payable to Savannah Symphony Women's Guild

Account Number   Expiration Date

Signature

Photocopies are accepted.